W9-BSX-226

PLANNING THE
PERFECT KITCHEN

BO NILES
and
JUTA RISTSOO

A Roundtable Press/Stonesong Press Book

SIMON AND SCHUSTER
NEW YORK   LONDON   TORONTO   SYDNEY   TOKYO

A Roundtable Press/Stonesong Press Book

Editor: Sheree Bykofsky
Managing Editor: Marguerite Ross
Assistant Editor: Martha Richheimer
Illustrations: Ray Skibinski
Template Illustrations: Norm Nuding
Cover and Interior Design: Michaelis/Carpelis Design Associates, Inc.
Front Cover Photograph: Copyright © David Arky
Front Cover Art: Courtesy of St. Charles, division of Whirlpool Kitchens, Inc. (left);
Poggenpohl USA Corp. (right)
Back Cover Photographs: Courtesy of Poggenpohl USA Corp. (top);
Quaker Maid (bottom)

Published by Simon and Schuster
A Division of Simon & Schuster Inc.
Simon & Schuster Building
Rockefeller Center
1230 Avenue of the Americas
New York, New York 10020

SIMON AND SCHUSTER and colophon are registered trademarks
of Simon & Schuster Inc.

10 9 8 7 6 5 4 3 2 1
Printed and bound in Singapore by Tien Wah Press Ltd.

Library of Congress Cataloging in Publication Data

Niles, Bo.
   Planning the perfect kitchen / Bo Niles and Juta Ristsoo.
      p.   cm.
   "A Roundtable Press/Stonesong Press book."
   Includes index.
   ISBN 0-671-65729-1
   1. Kitchens — Planning.   I. Ristsoo, Juta.   II. Title.
TX653.N56 1988
643'.3 — dc 19   87-32240

CONTENTS

INTRODUCTION 7

1. GETTING STARTED 9
Making a Scrapbook 9
Kitchen Profiles 10
Gathering Kitchen Ideas 14
Making a Rough Floor Plan 15
Working with Templates 18

2. ACTIVITY CENTERS 21
The Work Triangle 22
Traffic Patterns 23
Cooking Center 23
Food Preparation Center 25
Serving Center 26
Clean-Up Center 27
Refrigerated Foods Center 28
Supplementary Activities Centers 29

3. KITCHEN LAYOUTS 32
The One-Wall 32
The Corridor 33
The L-Shape 34
The U-Shape 36

4. CHOOSING APPLIANCES 38
Selecting Your Appliances 38
Range 39
Commercial Gas Range 41
Electric Wall Oven 42
Microwave Oven 43
Electric Cooktop 45
Gas Cooktop 47
Gas Wall Oven 47
Gas-Fired Barbecue 47
Exhaust Hood 48
Refrigerator/Freezer 49
Chest Freezer 52
Sink 52

Dishwasher 54
Trash Compactor 55
Garbage Disposal 56

5. STORAGE 57
Calculating Your Needs 57
Choosing Cabinets 58
Base Cabinets 58
Wall Cabinets 61
Specialty Cabinets 62
Open Storage 63

6. KITCHEN SURFACES AND
LIGHTING 66
Walls 66
Floors 69
Countertops 72
Ceilings 73
Lighting 74

7. WORKING WITH
PROFESSIONALS 76
Do I Need to Hire an Architect? 76
Should I Hire a Kitchen Designer
    Instead? 77
Do I Need a General Contractor? . . . 78
What If I Want to Subcontract
    My Own Job? 79

8. PLANNING THE BUDGET 80
Establishing a Budget 80
Allocating Expenses 80
Getting Bids 82

Directory of Resources 83
Index 95
Metric Conversion Chart 96
SCALED PEEL-AND-STICK
    DESIGNER TEMPLATES

INTRODUCTION

The kitchen is the heart of the home — the most important room in the house It is there that we cook, we eat, we entertain, and we talk over the day's events. It's the room that draws us together, the room where children gravitate for snacks and play, the room that nourishes us and comforts us.

It is not surprising then to learn that the kitchen is the most important feature that home-buyers consider when purchasing a new home, as reported by over 82 percent of respondents in a survey by the National Association of Home Builders. Further, for those who opt to stay in their present homes rather than move, the survey reveals that the kitchen is the number one room to be remodeled. Americans spend billions in re-modeling dollars each year on the kitchen.

Because the kitchen is more and more becoming a multipurpose room, planning is more critical than ever before. Ideally, non-cooking activities should be able to go on, but without obstructing cooking activities, and everyone should feel comfortable doing what-ever he or she wants anywhere in the room.

This book is entitled *Planning thc Perfect Kitchen* because there are some basic rules, some basic measurements, and some basic functions that apply to any kitchen design. You should, of course, ask yourself just what style you like, and keep it in mind, but then concentrate on the kitchen plan, because once your kitchen plan is set — after the "skeleton" of the room is created so to speak — you will find that it is really easier and more fun to dress the room any way you please.

First, then, ask yourself the following questions:

- How much storage do I need?
- How much counter space do I need?
- What appliances do I want?

These are the basic considerations that will guide your plan. The decoration of the walls and floor, the lighting, and, finally, your personal accessories, will naturally follow. You will have a kitchen, at last, that will work well for you and will express your personal style, too. You will have a kitchen that you, and everyone who shares the kitchen with you, will enjoy, be comfortable in, and love.

There is no such thing as *the* perfect kitchen. If there were, every kitchen you came across would look the same, feel the same, and function in the same way.

There is, however, a perfect kitchen for *you:* a kitchen that will look the way you want it to look, and function in a way that is comfortable and convenient for you.

This book has been written and organized to lead you to your own perfect kitchen. First of all, the book will tell you what you need to know about selecting appliances, countertops, flooring, and lighting, and it will counsel you on working with professionals. The book includes some tips on budgeting for a new kitchen and for remodeling an old one.

At the end of the book you will find three pages of templates, or scaled outlines, of the most common appliances, cabinets, and architectural features in the kitchen. You will use these as you develop your own plan for the kitchen of your dreams.

Information on actual planning and how to make a plan and on various kitchen layouts will help you visualize how you can work with the templates yourself. Clues on activities and storage space and how much room to plan for countertops will clarify spatial needs.

The inside back cover, which unfolds and lies flat, has been laminated and displays a grid of the same scale as the templates — 1/4 inch equals a foot. Using a grease pencil, you can draw the rough or final outline of your kitchen plan directly on the laminated cover and wipe it off with a tissue and start all over again. The templates, made of electrostatic vinyl, enable you to experiment with various floor plans on the grid. You can remove the templates and use them again and again, as often as you wish, as your plan evolves.

Because your plan will be to scale, you can show it to your architect, contractor, or kitchen planner; sharing this plan will insure that the kitchen you are dreaming of will turn out to be a reality.

1 GETTING STARTED

One of the clearest ways to begin to visualize your perfect kitchen is to make a scrapbook. Keep in it clippings and photos of kitchens and kitchen products that appeal to you. Also, keep a separate section to use as a notebook to jot down all of your ideas regarding your perfect kitchen as well as other information such as your responses to the profiles that follow this section.

MAKING A SCRAPBOOK

Buy a loose-leaf binder or a photo album with acetate sheets that fold back. You can add pages to a loose-leaf binder and you can move photos around under acetate sheets; either scrapbook option will give you enough flexibility to change your mind or expand upon your ideas as you go along. Also, a scrapbook will prove very helpful to you when you discuss appliance choices with your architect, contractor, or salesperson.

There are six basic areas of concern that you should make chapters for in your album.

These include the following:

1. *Layout.* This is the general arrangement of the room, including placement of appliances, cabinetry, and furnishings.
2. *Traffic patterns.* How you are able to move through the room is of paramount importance. You don't want to set up obstacles, nor do you want to make it difficult to perform any task. You also don't want to take too many steps from one area to another.
3. *Appliances.* The choices you make will affect the whole plan, since you will have to place your appliances so that they will function most efficiently and conveniently for you and for anyone else using them.
4. *Storage.* The positioning of cabinets and other storage spaces is vital to the organization of the kitchen. Most kitchens do not have enough storage, it seems, and many older kitchens did not place storage where it counts the most in terms of convenience. If you want everything to have its place, you will have to think a great deal about your storage needs.
5. *Lighting.* How well you see what you

are doing is very important; you will want to consider both general and specific lighting sources. You want a good ambient light, but you need to target particular areas or zones in the room, also.

6. *Surfaces.*   Many people consider walls, floor, and countertops to be decorative, but your surfaces should be easy to maintain, easy to clean, and visually appealing.

Consider adding the following to your scrapbook:

- A photo document of your present kitchen (if you are remodeling). Take snapshots of every wall, in sequence, to create a photo panorama of your old kitchen. The photos should show all of the problem areas at a glance. This visual aid will be immensely useful to the architect or contractor who will be working on the space.
- Shopping lists. As you make your purchases, both large and small, you may want to keep a record. You can tally up your costs, but you can also write in warranty and serial numbers and other information that could be crucial later on if you have to make repairs or replace anything.
- Telephone directory. You can list all service representatives on this page and people to call in case of an emergency.
- Style sheet. On this page you can note any style information regarding surface materials, such as wallcoverings. This quick reference guide will come in handy if you want to match up a piece of wallcovering or plastic laminate or whatever.
- Doodle pages. Plain pages kept just to doodle on are fun to include; many good ideas are derived from quick notes, sketches — and doodles!

Don't think of your album as complete at any time; you and your family will want to add ideas and notes throughout the process of conceiving, designing, and building the kitchen. And, finally, when it is all over and you are all settled in your new kitchen, you can look back at the scrapbook as a record of its "birth."

KITCHEN PROFILES

Your perfect kitchen begins — as it will end — with you. Your thoughts and your needs will dictate what you will want from your kitchen and just what it will do for you.

To get your ideas rolling, here are several short profiles that will lead you through the aspects of your lifestyle, your concerns, and your habits as they directly apply to living and working in the kitchen.

As you answer in your notebook the questions in the profiles, do the following:

- Jot down any additional ideas that occur to you as you go. Be sure to save all of your ideas!
- Ask everyone else who will actively share the kitchen with you to look at the profiles, too. You may be surprised at some of the answers you receive, and you may be astonished at everyone's separate set of priorities. Keep everyone's answers with your own. A kitchen that is well designed should incorporate the needs of everyone who will use it. If your kitchen perfectly suits you and also perfectly suits the ones you love, then you will all have a truly perfect kitchen, one that you, and they, will love.

Structural Profile

- Is your house all-new or old?
- Is it a single-story house, or does it have more than one story?
- What are the exterior walls made of?
- What is the roof made of?
- Are the actual kitchen walls made of drywall, plaster, cinder block, brick, or wood?

Is the floor made of concrete or wood?

Is there a floor covering currently in place?

Is the construction of the ceiling flat, peaked, or beamed?

Where are the doors and windows?

Can you, or will you, move the doors, windows, or walls?

Can you, or will you, move the plumbing lines, electricity lines, or gas lines?

Will you have more than one breakfast nook, dining area, counter area, or island in the kitchen?

Will you extend to or add on a family room?

Although these questions may appear to apply only to a remodeling project, they are good to consider if you are planning an all-new kitchen from scratch as well. The structure and materials of the background of the kitchen are what will support everything that goes into the room, and may, indeed, dictate those later decisions.

Often many of the new ideas you will have about a kitchen will derive from problems you have had with an old kitchen. List in your notebook all of the problems you can think of.

You may consider many other ideas fantasies you thought you'd never be able to afford to implement. Maybe you will be able to afford them now, though, if you plan properly. So, list all of your fantasy ideas in your notebook.

Ask the other members of your family, or those who will share your kitchen with you, to answer all of these questions, too.

Personal Profile

How tall are you?

How tall is everyone else who will use your kitchen often?

Are you left-handed or right-handed?

What is the distance from your elbow (bend your arm at a right angle to your waist) to the floor?

How high can you reach, comfortably?

How far can you reach (across a kitchen island or a table) comfortably?

How far can you reach when you are bending over?

COUNTERTOP STORAGE AND DISPLAY

Which of the following do you want to keep out on your countertop?

☐ Canisters
How many and
for what use
(e.g. flour, sugar,
coffee, tea,
rice, other)?
☐ Tea caddy
☐ Cookie jar
☐ Vitamins
☐ Spice rack
☐ Knife rack

☐ Dish rack
☐ Wine rack
☐ Wooden utensils
(in a jug, crock, or
other container)
How many and what
types (e.g. spoons,
mallet, rolling pins,
spaghetti tongs,
rubber spatula,
scoop, etc.)?

☐ Napkin holder
☐ Flatware caddy
☐ Paper towel rack
☐ Salt and pepper shakers
☐ Pepper grinder
☐ Sugar shaker
☐ Honey pot
☐ Dog biscuits
☐ Chopping block
☐ Mortar and pestle
☐ Food timer

WALL AND RACK DISPLAY

Which of the following would you like to display on your walls?

- ☐ Frying pans
- ☐ Saucepans
- ☐ Other pots and pans
- ☐ Colanders
- ☐ Strainers
- ☐ Measuring cups
- ☐ Salad spinner
- ☐ Muffin tins
- ☐ Flour sifter
- ☐ Food mills
- ☐ Graters
- ☐ Funnels

- ☐ Corkscrew
- ☐ Bottle/can openers
- ☐ Scissors
- ☐ Poultry shears
- ☐ Vegetable peeler
- ☐ Vegetable brush
- ☐ Metal utensils
  (e.g. slotted spoon,
  serving spoon,
  whisks, etc.)
- ☐ Cutting boards
- ☐ Breadboards

- ☐ Molds
- ☐ Trivets
- ☐ Knife rack
- ☐ Spice rack
- ☐ Spoon rack
- ☐ Potholders or oven mitts
- ☐ Paper towel rack
- ☐ Matchbook caddy
- ☐ Calendar
- ☐ Bulletin board
- ☐ Message board
- ☐ Clock
- ☐ Aprons

Would you like to hang any of the following from an overhead rack?

- ☐ Pots and pans
- ☐ Bunches of herbs

- ☐ Hanging baskets for
  foods, such as onions
  and potatoes

- ☐ Garlic strand
- ☐ Sausages

- Is it comfortable for you to squat?
- Does fluorescent lighting bother your eyes?
- Do your feet bother you when you stand for long periods of time?
- Can you lift heavy objects easily and without strain?
- Can you share your cooking area patiently and happily with others who may be cooking at the same time?
- Can you cook while unrelated activities are going on in the kitchen, or do you prefer to work undisturbed?
- Who actually does most of the cooking in your kitchen?
- Who does most of the cleanup?

Cooking Profile

- When you cook, do you clean up everything you use as you go along, or do you leave everything to be cleaned up when you are through?
- Do you follow recipes "to the letter," or do you improvise?
- Do you tend to prepare the same kinds of meals over and over, or do you constantly try out new recipes — and experiment?
- Do you cook with fresh, seasonal ingredients, or do you rely on supermarket staples?
- Do you serve packaged foods, or do you prepare from scratch more often?

Do you keep junk food on hand?

Do you often have food delivered to your home?

Do you like preparing raw foods (i.e., dicing, slicing, julienning, etc.)?

Do you do any specialized cooking, such as smoking, preserving, or canning, or using a wok or microwave oven?

Meal-Time Profile

Of the following, what kinds of meals do you and your family prefer?

Meals-in-minutes
Quick one-dish meals
Salads
Sandwiches and soups
Oven-cooked meals
Top-of-the-stove meals
Microwave cookery specials
Ethnic specialties
Stockpots, stews, and casseroles
Roasts
Steamed vegetables
Stir-fried foods

Do you bake often?

Do you serve baked goods often?

Do you prepare snacks, or do you keep packaged snacks around instead?

Do you eat multicourse meals?

Entertaining Profile

Do you eat out often?

How often do you entertain?

Do you usually entertain informally or formally?

How many people do you usually entertain on any given occasion?

Do you like to have sit-down dinners, buffets, luncheons, cocktail parties, barbecues, pot-luck meals, B.Y.O. or other special occasion parties?

Do you entertain in your kitchen?

Do your children entertain in the kitchen?

Do you enjoy having your guests in the kitchen while you cook?

Other Kitchen Activities Profile

What activities that don't involve cooking do you enjoy in your kitchen?

Watching evening news and/or morning TV
Monitoring children's homework or other projects
Talking on the telephone
Planning family outings and other events
Talking around the table or at the counter
Doing the laundry
Doing craft projects such as making holiday ornaments or presents
Grooming pets
Potting and caring for plants
Serving drinks to guests in the kitchen

Which of the following electronic aids and appliances would you consider vital to the comfortable functioning of your kitchen? Where applicable, which would you keep in the open to use all of the time and which would you store away for occasional use?

Wall telephone	Hand mixer/whisk
Tabletop telephone	Bowl mixer/
Telephone	attachments
answering	Food preparation
machine	center, countertop
Home sentry or	or built-in
burglar alarm	Drink mixer
system	Juicer
Smoke alarm	Extractor
Pre-programmed	Ice-cream machine
appliance control	Yogurt maker
system	Coffee grinder
Intercom	Spice grinder
Personal computer	Coffee mill
Automatic garage	Popcorn popper
door controls	Pasta machine
Radio	Waffle iron
Television	Electric frying pan
Air conditioner	Electric griddle

Fan
Coffee maker
Electric kettle
Espresso machine
Toaster
Toaster oven
Countertop
  microwave oven
Countertop
  convection oven
Combination
  toaster/microwave
  oven
Blender
Food processor

Electric wok
Slow cooker
Ice crusher
Can opener
Knife sharpener
Electric knife
Combination
  can opener/knife
  sharpener
Hand vacuum
Electric scrubber
Iron
Clock
Other

GATHERING KITCHEN IDEAS

If a new or remodeled kitchen has been on your mind for some time, you have probably already been consciously — or unconsciously — registering ideas all along. When you have visited a friend's house, for example, did you ask yourself: "Now, what do I like about this kitchen? What do I hate?" Personal reactions, spoken or unspoken, are actually ideas in disguise.

Every time you visit a kitchen, then, keep on asking yourself those two questions: "What do I like? What do I dislike?"

Then, when you are there (if you can) or when you return home, write down in your notebook the answers to those questions. "I really just loved that wood stove! That breakfast nook was really cozy! What a terrific cooktop!" or "Ugh, I hated the wallpaper; it was too busy! I'd never put my wall ovens that close to where the kids would play!" And so on . . .

Have you ever visited a decorator's show house? These are usually grand old mansions which are completely decorated, room by room, by a variety of designers who want to show off their skills and style. There are always

one or two kitchens to view, often replete with the newest appliances, newest surface materials, and latest gadgets. Designers want to win clients through these settings, so they go all out to demonstrate that they know what is the best solution to a space and how it should look. Lists of their sources are typically posted near the entrance of each room; in addition, the program guide to the show house will list the resources, both manufacturers and tradespeople, who were involved with each room.

Look at how department stores and specialty shops display their wares. You can garner some spectacular storage ideas from store displays. And you may become enthralled with a particular set of pots and pans or a beautiful set of dinnerware at the same time!

The easiest way to compile ideas, though, is to clip or note photographs and articles in magazines that feature kitchens on a regular basis. Magazines that specialize in kitchen design come out periodically, usually once or twice a year. Look for these on your newsstand or in your supermarket. Other magazines, commonly called "shelter books," such as *Metropolitan Home* or *House Beautiful,* devote their editorial content to architecture and interior design. Some shelter books publish a special remodeling section at least once a year. Many shelter magazines typically feature kitchens every month as well.

The "women's service" magazines such as *Good Housekeeping, Woman's Day,* and *Family Circle* run columns on new products and they sometimes highlight new appliances and new building products, too. These magazines dedicate their decorating and home-building pages to kitchens once a year, but they show kitchens in homes more often.

All of these magazines — special interest, shelter, and women's service — run advertisements from manufacturers of kitchen products so that you can see photographs and learn a bit about the newest introductions into the marketplace. Major and small appliances, kitchen cabinets, sinks, countertop surfaces, and the like are among the products you will see advertised. Look to see if an ad incorporates a coupon that you can clip and mail to receive more detailed information on the product or products featured. Many manufacturers will also send along a listing of dealers in your area who may have a showroom where you can view their products firsthand.

As you cut and clip, circle any descriptions that appeal to you. Look through the "Shoppers' Guide" at the back of each magazine; there you should find more details about products. At the end of this book, too, you will find a Directory of Resources listing manufacturers by category (e.g., Appliances), with their addresses and toll-free numbers.

If you do not want to cut up your magazines, you can photocopy the pages that you want to remember. The one problem with this is that, unless you use an expensive color photocopier, you will have no feeling of the colors of the room or product you are trying to recall. Make note, therefore, of the colors, and don't forget to take down the page numbers and the issue dates of the magazines in case you want to refer back to the original pages later on.

One huge guide that has proved invaluable to pros and nonpros alike is the *Sweet's Catalog. Sweet's* logs hundreds of brochures in detail, by category and by manufacturer. Check your local library for this resource. If you will be working closely with a professional architect, designer, or contractor, ask if the office has a *Sweet's* on hand and ask to look through it for ideas.

Your *Yellow Pages,* too, is a great resource. In it you will find dealers and showrooms to visit in your area. Displays of appliances can be seen at some department stores, too, as well as at the bigger home centers. At any of these places, ask for brochures to take home

and study. You might take a camera with you, too, to take photographs of setups you particularly like, if this is permitted. Finally, check with your local lumberyard and hardware store; these merchants will be able to give you tips to think about.

Everywhere you go, remember:

- Ask as many questions as you can.
- Take notes.
- Take brochures and any other giveaway materials.
- Make lists.

MAKING A ROUGH FLOOR PLAN

A rough floor plan will be the most important tool for visualizing a new or improved kitchen scheme. Such a plan consists of the basic outline of the room with all of its elements accurately measured out along its perimeter. Along with a photo document of your existing kitchen, the rough plan shows, clearly and distinctly, the space you have to work with, its obstacles or impediments — and its possibilities for improvement.

A rough plan is critical to an all-new design, too, but the features, of course, can be drafted from scratch, with no — or few — compromises.

Gridded surfaces, scaled 1/4 inch to a foot, are provided on the inside covers of this book. You can sketch right onto these covers with a grease pencil, which can be erased with a soft cloth or paper towel. If you want to make permanent copies of your sketches, to save and to refer to, you can buy gridded paper, by the sheet or in pad form, at your stationery or art supply store. Be sure to ask for the kind that is set up for designers and architects and is, like the grid on the cover, scaled 1/4 inch to a foot. If your kitchen is to be very large, you may have to tape two or more gridded pages together to give yourself enough space to work on. The inside back cover of

THE ROUGH FLOOR PLAN AND KITCHEN LAYOUT

Although the rough floor plan is only a sketch, it must be drawn up accurately in terms of the overall dimensions of the space because this outline is the basis for your ultimate floor plan. The openings and lines for power and plumbing also should be accurately positioned on the rough. Sketching the layout in rough form helps you visualize just how much space you have to work with. If you want to make major changes, the roughs are where you begin. You can see instantly what will be easy to move and what will be impossible to relocate.

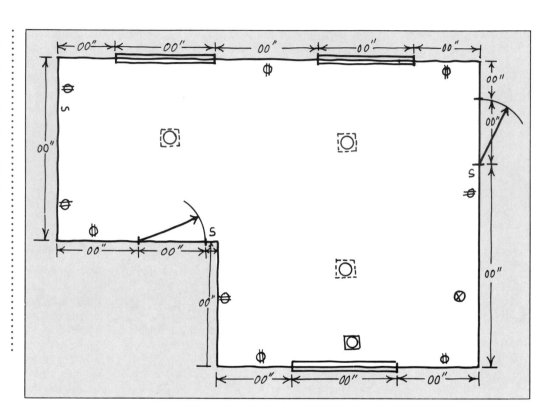

this book can accommodate even the largest kitchens and eating areas. If you use the entire gridded surface, your kitchen would measure 72 x 37 feet — large enough for a hotel installation and larger than many homes.

The scaled grid will be used over and over, through the various stages of design, until the final blueprints and working drawings are drafted up. The final blueprints or working drawings tell the builder everything that will go into the kitchen; every piece of lumber will be specified, every bit of hardware, every electrical wire — literally everything behind the walls, under the floor, and in the ceiling as well as everything out in the open. For your purposes now, though, the scaled grid should simply act as the background for your plans, those you will show to your architect, designer, or contractor.

Measurements of the room must be rendered exactly — to 1/16 of an inch. If you do not measure precisely, you can throw off the entire scheme. Appliances and cabinets are designed for a perfect fit; it would be a disaster to mismeasure and then purchase a particular piece that does not fit.

You will need the following in order to draw up the rough floor plan:

- A 6-foot folding carpenter's rule
- A retractable steel rule
- Sharp pencils and paper and a straight ruler

The carpenter's rule is the most accurate tool, but a retractable steel rule can be used

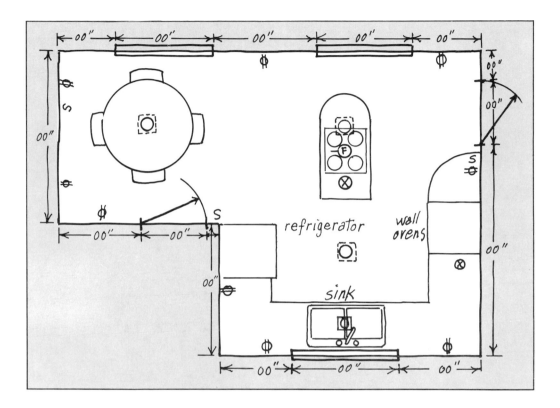

for window trim and other smaller dimensions without throwing off the fractional inch count.

Your first step in drafting the rough plan is to draw the actual perimeter, or outline, of the room. You will be calculating the overall dimensions of the space, and you will be establishing the configuration of the space.

Now roughly sketch the very basic perimeter of the room in light pencil. This "ghost" outline will act as a skeletal armature for the more exact measurements you will have to place along the edges of the room. You will ascertain, in advance, just what the overall length of each wall is. When you add up all the smaller dimensions, these figures will confirm the accuracy of your count.

Then, start again at one corner of the room

and measure the distance to the first opening or first obstruction you come to. This could be a jog in the wall or a window or a door. If it is a window or a door, measure to the outer edge of the trim first, then add the trim itself, then measure across the opening of the window or door, then continue across the trim again to complete the series of measurements.

Proceed in this manner all the way around the perimeter of the room. Be sure that you indicate every single obstruction as you go. When you have finished, add up all of the dimensions along each wall; opposite walls should match. If not, you will have to remeasure to correct your error.

Once you have calculated all of the overall measurements, you should jot down the heights

ROUGH FLOOR PLAN CHECKLIST

Structural features that can be moved:
- ☐ Doors
- ☐ Windows
- ☐ Walls

Features that can be moved:
- ☐ Location of the sinks
- ☐ Location of electrical outlets and switchplates
- ☐ Built-in lighting fixtures
- ☐ Location of heating/cooling units
- ☐ Door swings, either left or right, sliding, or pocket

Appliances that cannot be moved:
- ☐ Sink, if there is only one water line
- ☐ Gas range, because of gas line

Be sure to include the following vertical measurements in the margin of your floor plan:

- ☐ Vertical dimension from floor to ceiling
- ☐ Distances from floor to bottom of windowsills
- ☐ Distances from bottom of windowsills to top of window, including trim
- ☐ Height of doors
- ☐ Distances from floor to any soffits over existing cabinets
- ☐ Distances from floor to light switchplates

of the windowsills from the floor, and you should indicate how doors open and where they lead to.

You should indicate where the plumbing lines come in, as well as gas lines and all electrical lines. If you want to move any of these, which is a costly proposition, you will have to obtain accurate renderings of existing lines for the architect or contractor to consider when designing a new scheme.

One last consideration: Many older homes have walls that lean, windows and doors that are not square, and jogs that are uneven. You should take any discrepancy into consideration. In the margin, keep track of how far off these measurements are, so that you can discuss them with your architect or contractor.

Once you have drawn up your rough floor plan, you will undoubtedly want to make photocopies of it to doodle on and to refer back to as the design process moves forward. You will probably give copies to your architect or contractor, even though a design professional will also make up a rough floor plan as a rule. Give copies to other members of your family to work with, too; everyone's input counts.

On a copy of your rough plan, circle the areas where you would — ideally — like to do all of the different things you need to do in your kitchen. Would you like to wash dishes under a big window? Would you like to eat in a breakfast nook, or at a counter, or both?

If your rough plan relates to an existing kitchen, would you like to move one or more of your activity centers to other locations? Do you like where they are now? It is extremely difficult to move a gas line or plumbing, but it is easy to add extra electrical hookups. Consider, too, the ventilation of the cooktop or range; ventilating is easier if the appliance is placed on an outside wall because odors, smoke, and moisture should be ventilated to the outside. And look, too, at doorways; try not to block yourself in by them.

WORKING WITH TEMPLATES

Templates, as you can see when you turn to the last three pages in this book, are representations of the various appliances, cabinets, and furnishings you will want to place on your kitchen plan. These templates are scaled to fit on the grids on the inside back cover; that is, they are drawn so that the 1/4 inch equals a foot scale. You will see, though, that they are captioned with their actual dimensions, and this will help you clarify in your mind just how much room each item that you want in your kitchen will require. Ranges, for example, vary in size from 20 inches to 48 inches in width. Pick the template for the range that you want, but be sure that you leave enough space for the appliance you choose to fit on your plan. Most appliances and cabinetry conform to standards, in both size and shape. To better acquaint yourself with these sizes, first measure your current existing appliances and cabinets. Use the list of appliances and cabinet sizes you come up with as a guide and consult this guide often as you begin to visualize other sizes and other options.

As you learn more about each appliance

COMMON SYMBOLS

Once you have learned the basic symbols used on a floor plan, you have an easy shorthand that you can use over and over. The symbols allow you to visualize the various components on the floor plan at a glance; the symbols, too, are a common language you will share with your architect, contractor, or kitchen planner.

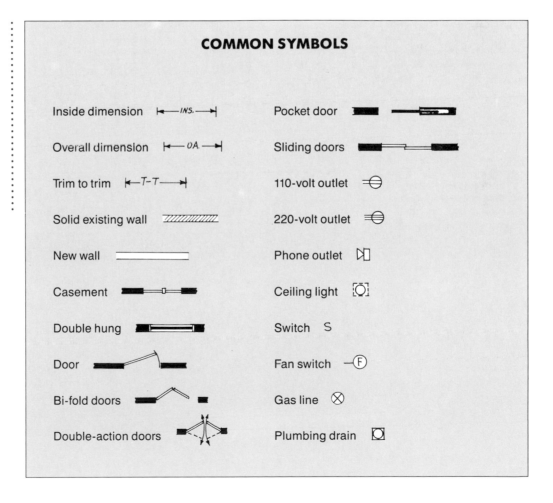

and about cabinet configurations, you may change your mind about what you really want to include in your kitchen. You may, for example (looking at the range again), decide not to have a range at all but to have a cooktop and separate wall ovens, instead.

Why not start playing with the templates now, even before you consult the rest of the book, just to familiarize yourself with sizes and shapes and possibilities. As you learn about all of the basic rules of kitchen design, you will gradually begin to refine your plan, and as you refine it, planning will become easier and easier.

MEASURING FLOORS AND WALLS

When you double-check the measurements of your kitchen, don't forget to check to see if your floor is level and walls are plumb. Even the slightest discrepancy can throw off the plan. To check floors, measure from the floor to the ceiling every 2 feet or so. Do all the measurements match? To check walls, measure diagonally from corner to corner on each wall. Does each pair of diagonals match? Do the diagonals of one wall match up with the diagonals of the opposite?

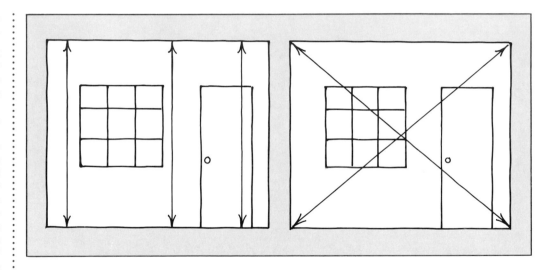

FLOOR PLAN DOUBLE-CHECK

1. Did you go over all your measurements at least *twice* to insure accuracy?
2. Did you figure on clearance on either side of each appliance for slide-in ease? (Figure on at least 1/4 inch on either side, except for the refrigerator, which needs extra breathing room — 1 inch on either side.)
3. Did you mark the *exact* location of plumbing, gas, and electric lines as well as wall switches?
4. Did you measure from wall to wall, and *not* from base molding to base molding? (Base moldings will throw off your count by at least an inch or two.)
5. Did you figure out if your walls or floor are uneven? (Measure from floor to ceiling in several spots to check if the floor is even. Measure each wall diagonally from corner to corner, and match up measurements to see if the wall is even.)

2 ACTIVITY CENTERS

Do you think of your kitchen simply as a place in which to cook? Your kitchen, in fact, encompasses a variety of activities, and if you look closely at each activity, you will find that each probably takes place in a certain part of your kitchen. For example, do you prepare vegetables on one counter and pull out foods from the refrigerator onto another? Is there a spot where you gather to eat breakfast or supper? Preparing foods, storing foods, and eating are all separate activities.

The basic activities in the kitchen — the preparation, cooking, and serving of foods; the storing of refrigerated foods; and the clean-up of foods, kitchenware, and dishes — are concentrated in three primary work zones, or "centers." Originally the food zone only focused on the cooking process, but as food preparation techniques have expanded to include preparation of fast foods, ethnic foods, snacks, and the like, this zone has been subdivided for efficiency.

The primary centers are anchored and revolve around a major appliance, or set of appliances, that function to facilitate and ease the workload. In the food area this appliance is the range or the cooktop, and it may be supplemented by wall ovens (which are usually situated away from the general activity area) or by other smaller cooking appliances such as a microwave or toaster oven. The refrigerated foods center, obviously, embraces the refrigerator and freezer, and the clean-up center takes its cue from the sink and dishwasher, although it may be supplemented by a trash compactor as well.

Each work center is also supplemented by the appropriate storage and countertop space so that you can comfortably use each center. How well each center functions and how well each interrelates with the others will be the difference between a well-designed and comfortable kitchen and one that is unpleasant to be in.

Supplementary centers, such as an eating area and a menu planning center, enhance the comfort of the room as a whole. These should integrate with the primary work centers but never obstruct them.

Before you plan any activity center down to

ACTIVITY CENTERS

When you look at your rough plan you can see that certain activities take place in certain areas of the kitchen. Make circles on the plan to locate these, or make notations to indicate each activity zone, or "center." How do the various centers relate to each other? Is there an overlap? Is the eating area, if there is one, located away from the food preparation area?

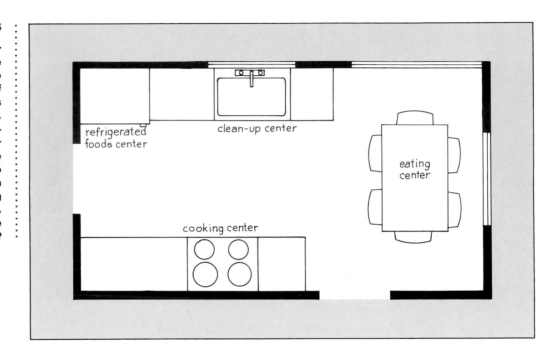

the last detail, read through the storage chapter, which outlines basic storage needs and gives some tips for making storage more efficient.

The critical rule, though, is: Keep supplies and utensils you will need for a particular task as close as possible to where you will work. This way you will find the items you need right at the outset without taking unnecessary extra steps. Also, place related activity centers next to each other. You will find your own comfortable pattern for working begin to evolve, and thus your work will become more organized and ultimately more pleasurable.

One tip: Stock just a week's supply of your staples at each work center and replenish these from a separate pantry or freezer where you keep items for long-term storage.

Think through the sequence of events for each task and try to repeat this sequence each time you repeat that particular task.

Establish routines. Establish rhythms. This will save you time and trouble and will leave you time for enjoying your accomplishments.

Some routines, such as cleanup, are so easy you can turn your mind onto "automatic," but others, such as recipe preparation, are more complicated. Give yourself enough room and time to enjoy each task, no matter how easy or how complicated.

THE WORK TRIANGLE

In old, inefficient kitchens, many steps were wasted traveling between various work areas and the eating area. In the 1950s, Cornell University initiated a series of studies which resulted in a revolutionary concept: Reduce the steps necessary for preparing and serving a meal by consolidating the primary work centers into a "work triangle." This triangle is measured from the center points of the kitchen's three primary appliances — the sink, the range, and the refrigerator. The sum of the three sides of the ideal triangle should not exceed 22 feet, nor should it be less than 12 feet. The specific distances between the three may vary according to any individual kitchen plan, but the total should fall within these parameters so that the cook will not waste energy.

TRAFFIC PATTERNS

For the work triangle to be effective, though, it should be compact and self-contained. Movement through the kitchen should not intersect with the triangle except when necessary. Every kitchen will have invisible "corridors" or traffic patterns passing through it, especially from one doorway to another. It is wise to locate the work triangle out of the path of any doorways, if possible.

As you plan your kitchen, think about all of your invisible corridors. How will you travel with your groceries from the back door to the refrigerator? Where will the children go when they come home from school? Who sets the table, and where are the dishes and condiments needed for a table setup?

Everything you do in the kitchen takes up room — opening a cupboard door, using an appliance, pulling out a chair or a bar stool — and all of these need space.

COOKING CENTER

When Cornell University first came up with the concept of dividing up the activities in the kitchen, labeling each as a work center, cooking was controlled by a single appliance in a single area — the range. Today you may still work at a single appliance — the range — but

THE WORK TRIANGLE

The primary work centers function best when they interrelate along a triangle, because this configuration reduces steps. The triangle, though, should be neither too large nor too small; its perimeter should equal between 12 and 22 feet. A Cornell University study found that this area is most comfortable for the average cook.

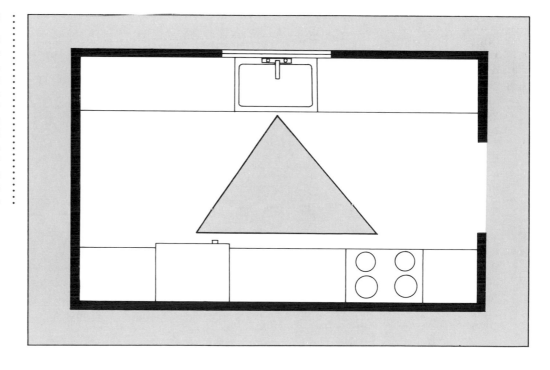

you can segregate various cooking tasks, too. You may choose to do your stovetop cooking at a cooktop and your baking and roasting in wall ovens. You may, in addition, use a microwave oven or a toaster oven — or both — for heating foods while performing highly specialized tasks in individual countertop appliances, such as an electric fry pan or wok or griddle.

Thus the cooking center may, indeed, be fragmented. Today the cooking center, as an element of your basic floor plan, refers to the area where you work at a cooktop. If the ovens are separate, they are usually located outside of the work triangle, and they are treated separately in the plan.

Before finalizing your floor plan, then, you should think through how you, and other members of your household, really cook. Perhaps you have already come to some conclusions after reading through the cooking profile. Ask yourself these elementary questions. Do you do a great deal of stovetop cooking, such as frying or sautéing? Do you do a great deal of oven cooking, such as roasting or baking? What, therefore, would be most practical and convenient for you: to utilize a single appliance or to separate your appliances? Do you want just a range, or would you prefer a combination of a cooktop and wall ovens?

The range or cooktop should have adequate countertop space on either side for flexible maneuvering of pot handles and lids. You need space on which to rest hot pots that have been removed from the cooktop; you also need space to spread out the utensils and food you will be working with. A bare minimum of 18 inches on either side allows you to turn pot handles away from the front of the cooktop, but you really need at least 30 to 36 inches on either side. This countertop allotment will merge with the food preparation

MAJOR TRAFFIC PATTERNS

You want to be able to move easily from one place to another in the kitchen and from the kitchen to other rooms in the house (and to the outdoors) without running into obstacles. Your movements form traffic patterns or corridors through the kitchen; these should not intersect with the work triangle because you don't want to impede food preparation or serving.

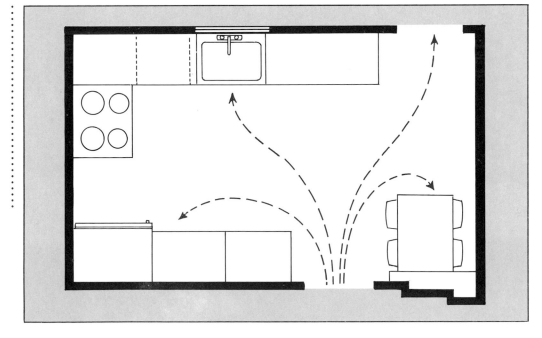

CLEARANCE FOR POT HANDLES

Because pot handles protrude beyond the edges of the cooktop or range, you must plan enough room on either side of the cooking appliance for them. Pot handles should always be turned away from the front of the range or cooktop so that you—or a child—will not tip the hot pot and cause an accident.

COUNTERTOP SPACE FOR PREPARING FOODS

For the preparation of foods, a minimum of 3 feet of counter space should give you enough room to set out utensils and ingredients, while allowing you enough room in which to work. This allotment is not liberal, but the food preparation center usually runs into the cooking center, thus increasing the overall length of the counter. If you share your counter with another person, then you will want to add another 2 feet of countertop space.

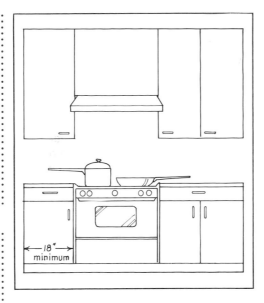

center and will probably connect with the sink area, too, in your overall scheme.

Utensils and foods used at the cooktop should be placed within easy reach. If you think through your basic recipes, you will see that certain ingredients probably appear again and again in your cooking and would no doubt be more convenient for you if kept nearby rather than in a faraway pantry. Consider keeping the pots and pans you use most often near the cooktop, too. Cooking tools should be close at hand, either in a drawer or in a crock, or hanging on the wall.

When you are working at the cooktop or range, you want to have enough room to move about and you also want to leave enough space for others to pass behind you as you work. A minimum of 38 inches gives you enough room to open the oven door of a range, but an allotment of 64 inches is better because it allows for easy traffic throughout the area.

A range or cooktop should never be positioned under a window, especially if powered by gas. Wind can extinguish the pilot light or

flame. Reaching across the cooking surface can be dangerous, too. Move the cooking center, therefore, at least 15 inches to either side of the window. Situating the cooktop or range on the window wall is, of course, best for the placement of a ventilating hood as odors and smoke can be sucked to the outdoors easily.

FOOD PREPARATION CENTER

The food preparation center, although not specifically focused on a single major appliance, is the area where you spend much of your kitchen work time. Logically, the stretch of countertop associated with food preparation should run between the cooking center and the sink because some foods must be prepared near the sink and many foods are transferred from the food preparation area to the cooktop or range.

What kinds of foods do you prepare most often: packaged foods or foods from scratch? Your cooking habits will affect your decisions

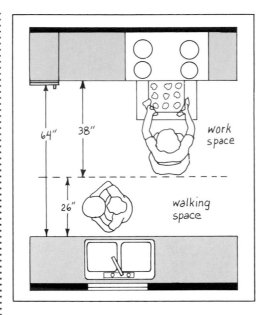

regarding the food preparation area as much,
if not more, than any decision concerning the
kitchen. You may require separate zones for
specific types of food preparation; you may
want to differentiate certain cooking tasks. For
example, do you need a big chopping block
for dicing, slicing, mincing, and chopping
foods? Do you need a separate slab of marble
or a polyester board for rolling out cookie or
pie dough? Do you need extra space for two or
more cooks to prepare foods simultaneously?

Food preparation, these days, is abetted by
a battery of small appliances, such as the
food processor, blender, meat slicer, and electric knife. Which of these might you want to
keep out on the countertop, and which can
be stored away between uses?

You need enough counter space — at least
36 inches, minimum — to accommodate the
small appliances you like to keep out, and
you may want additional room to store canisters
of most-used ingredients such as flour, sugar,
rice, and pasta. Consider installing an elec-

trical outlet strip along the wall behind the
counter so that each appliance can be plugged
into its own independent outlet.

The pots and pans you use at this center
should be stored as close to the center as
possible. Tools for mixing, slicing, stirring,
and other procedures should also be located
here. The foods that you use often, including
herbs and spices, shortening, oils and vine-
gars, packaged foods and some canned goods
will be within reach if they are stored over the
counter or nearby.

Depending upon the task you are performing,
you may want to vary the height of the counter
at the food preparation center. The standard
height for a countertop is 36 inches, but some
tasks, such as rolling out dough, are best
performed at a counter that is only 32 or 33
inches high. If you can, then, try to drop the
counter in the baking area, and keep it raised
at the chopping area.

Some cooks have the food preparation
center do double duty as the serving center
as well; if so, this area should be situated
near the eating area.

If the food preparation counter and serving
counter are on an island that's shared with a
cooktop and eating area, be sure to leave
enough room for dishes to be stacked along-
side any foods that are being prepared and
served.

SERVING CENTER

It is obviously most efficient to locate the serving
center close to where you will be eating, be it
at a countertop or at a table. If you do eat at a
counter, the serving center might naturally
extend from this area; at an island, part of the
food preparation area near a cooktop might
act as a serving center, too.

Do you want to use the serving center as a
buffet for entertaining? Do you want it to function as a repository for clean dishes before

COUNTERTOP SPACE FOR CLEANUP

Stacking dishes and pots and pans takes up quite a bit of room, so you should allot enough counter space on either side of the sink to carry the load. The absolute minimum on one side (if this counter runs up against a wall) is 18 inches; this leaves just enough room for a drain board to rest next to the sink. Better yet, leave 24 inches on either side of the sink. More is better. The sink counter will undoubtedly run into another center, probably the serving center, so at least one counter should be longer than 24 inches.

setting the table and for dirty dishes after eating? You will need at least 24 inches of counter space, but 37 inches will give you more latitude for setting out food and dinnerware at the same time.

You may decide to keep a toaster, coffee maker, or other small appliance out on the serving center, so be sure to equip the center with an extra electrical outlet.

At the serving center, dinnerware, serving pieces, and glassware used on a daily basis should find their niche. Table linens, flatware, and serving cutlery should be stored there, too, as well as trivets and insulated pads for hot pots.

Certain foods, usually taken directly to the table, could be wisely stored nearby. Salt and pepper, other favorite seasonings, sugar, cookies and crackers, dry cereals, honey and relishes, and vitamins are all most convenient to serve if they are kept at or near this center.

If you combine your food preparation and serving centers, you will need plenty of room to accommodate many utensils plus dinnerware and food. If so, you may want to keep

food in a nearby pantry to liberate some of the cabinet space. Just be certain you don't place the pantry so far away that you will be adding to your travel time between centers.

CLEAN-UP CENTER

The sink grouped with a dishwasher and, perhaps, a trash compactor and garbage disposal consolidates clean-up activity. Your choice of sink may be dictated by how much or how little you use a dishwasher. Your choice, too, may be based upon other chores you would perform at the sink, such as peeling vegetables, arranging flowers, or washing fabric items, such as dirty napkins. Sinks can run up to 4 feet wide, which gives you plenty of room to stack and soak pots in one bowl of a triple-bowl sink while rinsing dishes or foods in another bowl. But if your dishwasher is to take on all of the heavily soiled utensils as well as dishes, you may not need a sink that is any larger than a standard 24 inches wide. Some sinks, too, come with integral drain board extensions, and you must plan for this.

Do you use your sink for other functions? Do you cut and peel vegetables into the sink (and, therefore, need a garbage disposal underneath)? Do children use the kitchen sink for messy activities or for washing hands? Does the sink become the repository for anything dirty that happens to be in the room?

Sinks these days come with a wide array of faucets and fittings, including dispensers for hot and chilled water and pure drinking water, as well as a soap dispenser and a retractable spray arm. Be sure everyone in your household is familiar with the fittings you choose; a hot water dispenser, for example, could burn a small child.

The placement of the dishwasher should be both convenient and instantly accessible. For a right-handed person, the dishwasher is best placed to the left of the sink — and vice

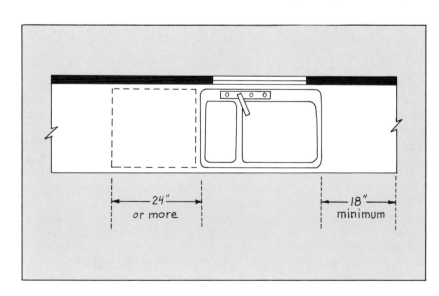

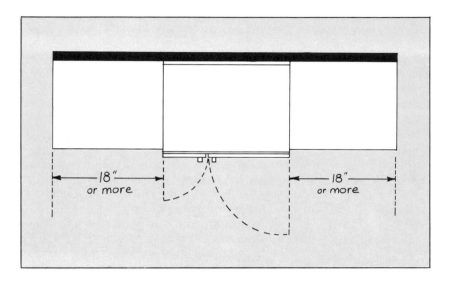

COUNTERTOP SPACE FOR REFRIGERATOR

When you park groceries next to the refrigerator, you will need at least 18 inches next to the open door (or next to each door if the appliance is a side-by-side model). This span will probably run into an adjoining work counter, at least on one side, to maximize the space on which you can place foods.

colanders, strainers, and salad spinners, are easy to reach when stored there along with the pots and pans they would be used with.

Many people place all of their household cleansers under the sink. This can be extremely dangerous in homes with small children or pets, and in such cases it would be best to store all poisonous provisions up high and out of reach while leaving buckets and sponges and safer items under the sink. Or put a child-proof lock on the cabinet to insure safety.

The nicest place to put a sink is right in front of a window so that you can look out while you are washing up. If you enjoy growing your own herbs, you might insert a small green-house window here so that you can reach across the sink and snip herbs when the mood strikes you.

versa. A trash compactor should be installed on the opposite side of the sink from the dish-washer, and a garbage disposal would lock into place under the drain in the sink.

You should allot equal amounts of room on both sides of the sink to accommodate dirty objects and clean ones. If you have a dish-washer alongside the sink, you already have 24 inches of countertop capping that appli-ance. Plan on at least 24 inches across the sink, but, better yet, allow at least 36 inches because the counter will undoubtedly run into the food preparation area or serving area or both. If two or more people share clean-up duties, be sure that there is plenty of room for everyone to maneuver around the sink.

Many people prefer to store all dinnerware and glasses that are used on a daily basis near the dishwasher rather than at the serving center. It's your option. Pots and pans and kettles that are filled with water before any food is added in a recipe can be grabbed most conveniently if they are kept near the sink or source of water. Utensils, such as

REFRIGERATED FOODS CENTER

Before you plan your refrigerated foods center, you should ask yourself these questions. How much food do you refrigerate and how much food do you freeze? Do you often store left-overs? Do you cook foods in large batches to freeze for a later date?

Some homeowners use the refrigerator much more often than a freezer and some, conversely, must have more than one freezer to store foods for long periods of time. Calcu-late your requirements. It is, after all, one thing to freeze a side of beef and quite another to put up a couple of ice cube trays and a con-tainer of ice cream!

The refrigerator/freezer is the largest appli-ance in the kitchen, but it actually requires the least amount of contiguous counter and cabinet space. You need only 18 inches along-side the door of the appliance; the door should open toward the counter for easy transferral of foods into the refrigerator and freezer com-partments. If you want a side-by-side type of refrigerator/freezer, you should plan on a minimum of 18 inches on either side — once again to make it easy to place foods into the appliance from the countertop nearest the door of the compartment.

The average refrigerator/freezer juts out past the standard 24-inch-deep base cabinet run. If you don't like this extra bulk, select an appliance that has been designed to be flush with the cabinetry. The newest so-called modular refrigerator and freezer components are actually separate appliances. You can stack these or place them side by side. The flexibility allows you to have as many compartments as you wish. The smaller versions even tuck in under the counter.

Try to store bags, containers, and wrappings used for storing foods nearby. If you select a refrigerator/freezer with in-door dispensers for crushed ice and chilled water, you may want to keep a horde of extra glasses close at hand, too.

SUPPLEMENTARY ACTIVITY CENTERS

To enhance the atmosphere of the kitchen, and add to its value, both in monetary terms and in terms of comfort and efficiency, there are several supplementary centers to consider incorporating. The first, and most obvious, is an eating area. Most homeowners want an informal eating arrangement in the kitchen, either at a counter or at a table — or both. Active families gather at one or both locations, and guests naturally gravitate toward these areas, too, because nothing is more enticing than the sight and scent of a home-cooked meal shared with family and friends.

Two other centers that more and more homeowners desire are a menu planning center and a separate entertaining center that may double as a bar.

Eating Center

To maximize the enjoyment of a kitchen, many people add on one or more eating areas to their general kitchen plan. The easiest solution is to extend one countertop, preferably the countertop on a peninsula or on an island. This extension cantilevers from the base cabinet so that stools can draw up underneath. Because countertops are 36 inches off the floor, stools must be used; if you don't like to sit this high, you can drop the countertop to a more comfortable height so that you can use chairs instead of stools. The common height for a table is 30 inches.

Along a counter, either on a peninsula or island, reserve 20 x 24 inches for each place setting. If your kitchen is small and your peninsula or island short, you may be able to reserve only two places.

A separate eating area takes up a disproportionate amount of space; the dimensions of an eating area, in fact, can equal that of the kitchen area itself. A round table to seat six, for example, must measure at least 42 inches to 48 inches in diameter, to give each diner enough room. But you have to add on enough space for chairs to pull out and for other people to pass behind the chairs when they are occupied. If you tally in a full seating — six people at the table — plus a walkway all around, that really adds up. You need 36 inches to pull a chair back, but 48 inches would be a more tolerable allotment for comfort of movement.

The walkway must be adequately wide if the counter or island stands across from a cabinet run and an appliance or tub. You must leave room to open the doors of these while someone is seated and another person is passing between.

Menu Planning Center

A desk, outfitted for menu planning with a recipe index and cookbook storage close by,

COUNTER HEIGHTS

Many kitchens call for an eating area at the counter— be it along a peninsula or at an island. The standard counter height, however, is 36 inches, so the countertop usually has to be adjusted, or you must buy stools that fit underneath. The lip of the counter must be extended to become a proper tabletop—at least a foot to 20 inches, depending on how you intend to use the counter. If you don't like to sit at a high counter you can drop the lip to the standard table height, which is 30 inches.

MENU PLANNING CENTER

A quiet nook for writing, phoning, and planning a menu is a luxury, but one demanded by many people these days. A 30-inch wide desk top is what you need; the height and depth of a desk is different from the height and depth of a cabinet, though, so you will have to plan a separate unit for this menu planning area. It is best, in fact, to design a whole area apart.

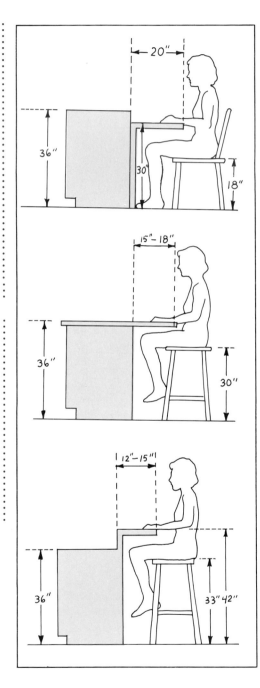

and a telephone with a message board, is simultaneously a center for planning meals and a command post for all sorts of family activities. Add a personal computer for keeping track of bills and for other tasks, and an intercom for keeping tabs on family members throughout the house, and you are all set!

Desks usually measure only 20 inches deep, as opposed to the standard base cabinet depth of 24 inches, and a desk top is 30 inches high — like a table — rather than the standard base cabinet height of 36 inches. If the desk extends from a cabinet run, then it must drop from 36 inches to 30 inches to be the right height and it must be cut back 3 inches to be just the right depth. Allow at least 24 inches side to side and, better yet, 30 inches, to give yourself enough room for desk-top necessities. If you do add a computer, though, you will need a surface of 48 inches in width for elbow room. An intercom can be built into the wall if the desk hugs a wall; if the desk is on a peninsula, the intercom will have to be located elsewhere.

**CLEARANCE FOR
DINING AREAS**

An eat-in kitchen is the ideal for many homeowners. A dining area, though, takes up a great deal of room. You must consider the table first of all, and then you must take into account how many people will eat there and how they will be able to move around the table when people are seated there. A corridor of at least 3 feet on each side of the table is a bare minimum. A round or oval table will garner a few precious inches; the corners of a square or rectangle eat up space.

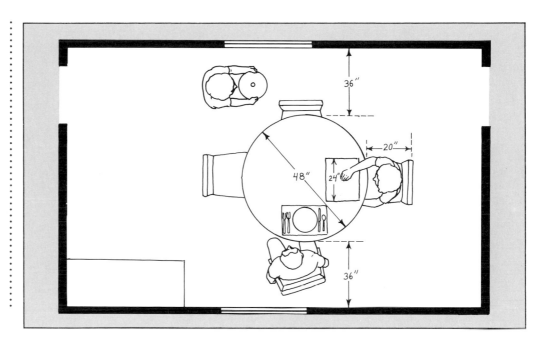

BAR/ENTERTAINING CENTER

A bar area proves immensely popular with those who entertain often, but this area requires quite a bit of space because of its allotment of appliances. Usually the bar setup includes an extra refrigerator, even if it is a narrow one, plus a dishwasher and a sink. A wine storage rack is a popular choice for this area, as is an ice maker. Allow at least 70 inches of space to accommodate all of these appliances, with countertops to match.

Bar/Entertaining Center

Adding a separate bar may seem like a pure luxury, but in large families — or if you entertain a great deal — this center can become as crucial to the enjoyment of the kitchen as any other area.

A bar area typically includes a bar-size sink. A supplementary dishwasher, for glasses and extra dishes, and a separate refrigerator add to the efficiency of this center. The refrigerator can tuck in under the counter with an ice maker beside it. All of these appliances will require a cabinet run of at least 70 inches; this will allow for a bit of storage under the counter as well. Of course you will have to add a plumbing line to this center to service all of these appliances.

Glass storage in overhead cabinets is a must here; you may also want to keep snack foods, trays, and special condiments in the cabinets.

3 KITCHEN LAYOUTS

Because the work triangle has proved itself to be the most efficient configuration of appliances and because it reduces steps, most kitchen plan designs derive from four basic layouts that incorporate the triangle: the pullman or one-wall kitchen; the corridor or two-wall kitchen; the L-shaped kitchen; and the U-shaped kitchen. Both the L and the U may expand to include a peninsula or an island for increased versatility. All of the layouts are adaptable to your needs; you will have to gauge how many extras you require in order to arrive at the plan of your choice. Do you want any extra appliances and, if so, where would you put them? How much extra storage space or counter space do you need?

THE ONE-WALL

Of all the layouts, the one-wall kitchen is the least efficient because it collapses the triangle and requires you to take extra steps to move between the two farthest points. In this layout there is little room for storage or counter space.

However, in many older homes and apartments, and in many new, tiny studio apartments, this is the only configuration possible.

The one-wall is a good choice as a supplementary kitchen because you do not have to add space for it; you do, of course, have to provide the electricity and plumbing necessary for the appliances.

A one-wall arrangement, like all of the kitchen layouts, should branch out from the sink. The one-wall should stretch at least 15 feet to be efficient, and the distance from the kitchen wall to the opposite wall should reach at least 72 inches to leave room for appliance doors to open; 96 inches is preferable to allow for people to pass while the cook is at work. Counters should reach at least 24 inches between appliances and 36 inches if possible, because 24 inches is really very tight for comfort. Also, leave at least 18 inches at either end of the one-wall for clearance between the appliances and the wall or access to the kitchen area.

If the one-wall faces an open room, con-

ONE-WALL KITCHEN

When space is at a premium, often the only solution to a kitchen plan is to place all of the appliances and cabinets along one wall. Try to separate appliances so that you will have counter space between them. One way to gain additional storage in this otherwise fairly cramped scheme is to extend wall cabinets all the way to the ceiling, thus gaining space taken up by the soffit.

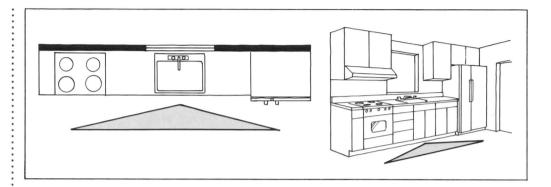

sider adding an island — even a roll-around version — to give yourself more work space. The island will function, in addition, as a room divider, and you can use it for extra storage, too.

THE CORRIDOR

Extending along two walls, the corridor kitchen makes good use of the work triangle when the three major appliances are positioned appropriately opposite to each other. Again, center this layout on the sink and place the refrigerator and range opposite with counter space between them. The corridor itself should reach at least 108 inches from wall to wall, since you will have doors opening from both directions in this layout, and you will need to leave room for traffic as well.

The corridor kitchen may open at both ends, but it is preferable to shut off one end so that

CORRIDOR KITCHEN

Stringing appliances and cabinets along two walls increases storage and counter space, even though the actual floor space is often quite cramped. Remember to leave enough room in the corridor itself for two people to pass each other comfortably. Traffic decreases substantially when one end of the kitchen is closed off.

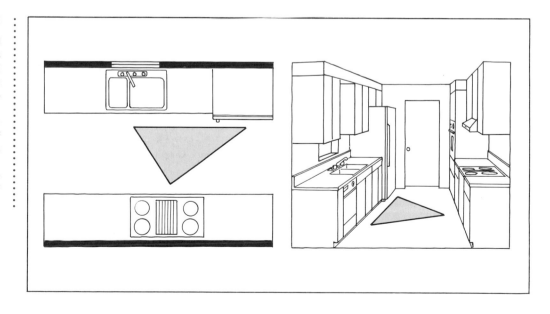

L-SHAPED KITCHEN

The two legs in an L-shaped kitchen can stretch on indefinitely, so their lengths are best determined by the placement of the appliances and the resulting work triangle. Keep in mind that the sum of the sides of the triangle should not exceed 22 feet. The cabinets and counters that extend on either side of the actual work triangle are best used for supplementary utensils and dishes; all supplies contained within the triangle should be those used most often so that they are easily accessible to the cook.

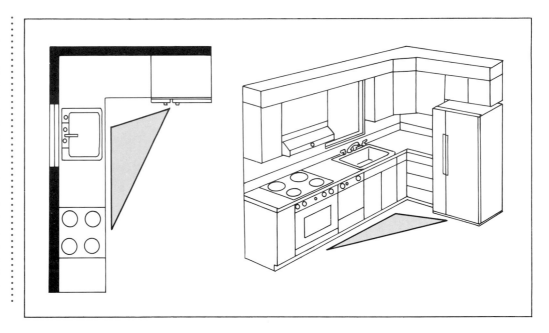

the corridor does not turn into a major "highway" from one area of the house to another. If the kitchen must remain open at both ends, widen it sufficiently to allow easy passage even when one or more people are working in the space.

Again, the sink centers the activities, but with the greater flexibility of the corridor layout you can add another, smaller sink for bar set-ups along that same wall or along the opposite wall, near the refrigerator.

Depending upon the length of the corridor, you can concentrate your wall storage along one wall or stretch it out along both walls.

THE L-SHAPE

The L-shape lends itself naturally to a work triangle by utilizing two adjoining walls or a wall and a peninsula. The most effective positioning of the appliances is to place the sink on a diagonal in the corner of the L with the range and refrigerator at the two ends of

the arms of the L. Placing the sink cater-cornered will allow you to maneuver easily in the corner, and you can place a garbage disposal under the sink, allowing plenty of room behind it for the plumbing hookup.

You can also use a "pie" sink in the corner. This is a sink that has two bowls split at a ninety-degree angle so that one bowl fits onto one arm of the L and one fits onto the other, with the fittings between the two.

The refrigerator traditionally stands at one end of the L. Be certain to specify a door opening that will face the counter next to the refrigerator. The range does not have to stand at the end of the other arm, and in fact should not, because the range functions best when hot-pot and serving counters flank it. As indicated in the discussion on activity centers, leave 36 inches on one side of the range for serving and for food preparation and 18 inches on the other for placing hot pots.

If you decide to turn the L into a peninsula,

L-SHAPED VARIATIONS

The L-shape adapts readily and handily to a variety of kitchen designs, and specifically to those that include a peninsula or an island. Often the appliance placed on the peninsula or the island is a cooktop, and serving foods to the eating areas takes place here. You can extend the peninsula or expand the island to include an eating counter, too, but you must be certain to leave enough room for the diners to eat comfortably without being too close to the hot cooktop.

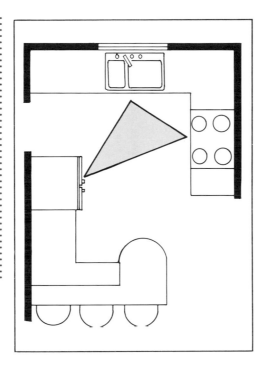

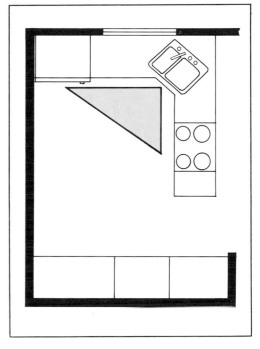

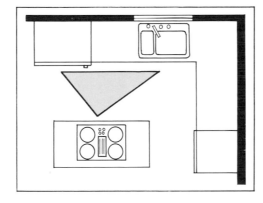

it is recommended that you position a cooktop on the peninsula with wall ovens located nearby but out of the work triangle. You can extend the peninsula into an eating counter; just be sure to leave plenty of room for serving as well as place settings for diners.

A NOTE ABOUT PENINSULAS

If your scheme must work around doors or accesses to the kitchen that cannot be closed off, the peninsula will prove a most convenient solution for attaining a separate work area. A peninsula will separate the cooking zone from major traffic patterns. The peninsula can be shaped or positioned in a number of ways; it need not stretch at a right angle, but can branch out into the room at a wider angle if desired. The peninsula can bend if you would like it to; it does not have to be straight. The peninsula may also function as a pass-through to an adjoining room, with storage convenient to both sides.

The favorite configuration by far, when there is enough space, is the U-shape because the work triangle can bounce off all three walls, or it may be enclosed within one portion of the U if the U also includes an island. The storage space and counter space are increased dramatically in this layout, which also allows plenty of room for several people to work in the kitchen simultaneously without bumping into each other.

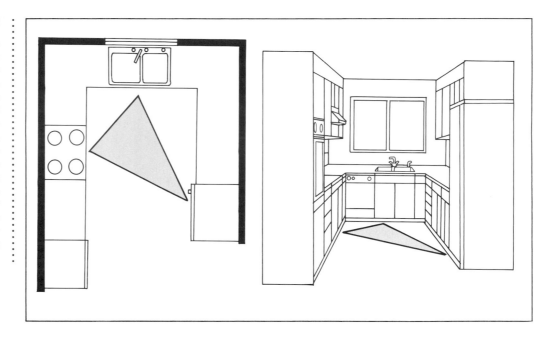

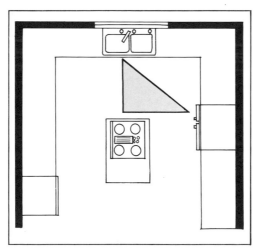

Do not attempt to create an L-shaped kitchen in a very small room because crowding of the appliances creates obstacles: When doors open, they bump into each other.

THE U-SHAPE

The U-shape, the most popular of all kitchen layouts, accommodates the greatest amount of storage and counter space while maintaining a convenient work triangle separate from other activities.

In the U, the sink is often located beneath a window and the work areas then radiate logically to the counters and down the arms of the U. Many U-shaped kitchens incorporate a peninsula into the scheme, and for increased flexibility, other, larger U-shaped kitchens will add an island between the two arms of the U.

The smallest U-shaped layout should have a base of at least 96 inches; 10 to 12 feet is preferable, however, to widen the work area contained within the arms of the U. The arm of the U accommodating the refrigerator should run at least 48 to 60 inches in length and the arm embracing the range, or cooktop, should stretch at least 66 inches.

A NOTE ABOUT ISLANDS

For an island to function well, it should measure at least 24 inches by 78 inches, leaving enough room for a cooktop and adequate counter space surrounding it. If you want to eat at the island but do not want to increase the size of the base, you can add a lip.

Remember that electricity must run to the island and, if you do not select a down-draft vent option, you will have to install a ventilating hood overhead. As many people consider a hood an obstacle, be sure to calculate the size and shape when you place one over the island.

If you can include a large island in your scheme, consider adding a second small sink here to facilitate cleanup.

MAKING A LIST OF APPLIANCES FOR YOUR LAYOUT

When you think about your perfect layout, list all of the major appliances you wish to include, especially if you want to duplicate appliances. Big families, for example, often need two dishwashers. And if you entertain a great deal, you may want an extra ice maker and an extra trash compactor integrated into your scheme. Conversely, if you are working with a small space, you may want to eliminate a particular appliance, or find one that is smaller than the norm. There are dishwashers, for example, that tuck away under the sink.

After you make your list, write down all of the sizes and shapes of the appliances, and calculate your countertop needs. Do you want wide or narrow appliances? The templates in this book represent the standard sizes, so you will have to alter the templates or draw your own if your selections do not match up.

4 CHOOSING APPLIANCES

Each year, at the National Association of Home Builders (NAHB) Show and again at the Kitchen and Bath Show, companies who manufacture major kitchen appliances introduce their newest models "to the trade." At these shows — or conventions — thousands of builders, contractors, and designers review all that is current in this field, which is expanding as more and more European companies are bringing their appliances into the American marketplace. As a result, American manufacturers are picking up on European styling and technology.

Electronic controls enhance many major appliances, especially the top-of-the-line models. Such innovations as touch controls, readouts, and message centers are becoming more commonplace and "user friendly," and, as a result, are increasingly in demand. With time, such innovations will become standard on lower-priced models, too. If you choose appliances with "bells and whistles," be sure to train each member of your household to operate them.

Styling today leans toward the understated. Although manufacturers are not giving up on enamel finishes, they are moving in the direction of sleek black glass, which harmonizes with any decor, from ultra high-tech to down-home rustic. Many manufacturers offer "trim kits." These are separate frames that accommodate thin panels of any material you choose (most consumers opt for panels that match their cabinetry) and can lock onto the front of the appliances.

Stainless steel, considered the most "professional" look for kitchens, is less in evidence as an all-over finish, probably because it requires a tremendous amount of upkeep to retain its luminosity. Stainless, however, is still the preferred material for sinks.

SELECTING YOUR APPLIANCES

When you begin to select appliances, consider, of course, the overall look of your kitchen, but more importantly, think through your cooking habits thoroughly. Do you, in fact,

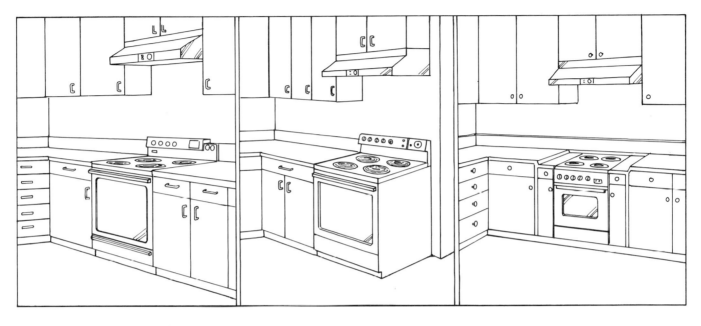

RANGE

The standard four-burner range is available in three options, depending upon installation. As a free-standing unit, the range is finished on the sides—in case one or both sides will show. The built-in version is fully insulated, but the sides are not finished off with side panels because these would not show. Eliminating the panels assures a snug fit between the base cabinets. The drop-in range does not reach to the floor; instead, it fits into a specially-constructed base cabinet outfitted with a drawer and toeplate underneath.

need all of the high-tech gadgets and gizmos? Just what features on each appliance will benefit you — and your family? Ask to see brochures and read them thoroughly. Examine each appliance, feature by feature, and then see how each appliance relates to the other appliances in the kitchen. The capabilities of one appliance should enhance and be enhanced by the others. For example, if you prepare foods in large quantities for future use, you will want to have a range — or cooktop and wall ovens — equipped with enough burners for cooking in this manner, and you will want a refrigerator with a freezer large enough to accommodate what you will want to store.

RANGE

Although many cooks prefer to separate top-of-the-stove activity from ovens, the full-feature range is still the cooking appliance of choice for most households because it consolidates all cooking activities in one appliance and is compact. Many kitchens simply cannot accommodate separate cooking appliances because of spatial restrictions.

You can choose a range in one of three types. The free-standing range is finished on the sides so that, if necessary, it can be placed at the end of a cabinet run. The built-in range, without side panels, slides right between base cabinets. The drop-in range drops into a cabinet run, sharing the toeplate, and, typically, has a below-the-oven drawer that coordinates with the cabinetry on either side.

Ranges vary in size. The smallest, just 20 inches wide, is selected mainly by home builders or developers for small apartments. The two most common sizes are the 30-inch and the 36-inch-wide varieties. The 30-inch, in fact, is considered the "standard," and most kitchen plans specify this size. The 48-inch-wide size is indicated for the commercial gas range developed primarily for restaurant use.

The range may operate on gas or on electricity. If you already have a gas line in your kitchen, it is probably best to use it for your new gas range. Many cooks prefer a gas cooktop because they feel they can control the accuracy of the flame. In houses with small children, gas is a wise choice because you can see the flame when the burner is on. The newest gas ranges offer the safety feature of pilotless ignition, but this feature requires a separate electrical hookup. The benefit of pilotless ignition is that there is no flame in the pilot light cavity except when it is ignited, and so your gas costs are reduced.

The electric range is increasingly versatile and now boasts burner controls as accurate as gas. The so-called "Eurostyle" solid element burners are being selected more and more over the conventional electrical coil because they heat up more evenly and, once warmed up, respond more quickly to touches of the controls. Thermal sensors centered on the discs change color when the element is on so that you can monitor the heat. With both conventional electric coils and discs, however, there is a danger to children; when the range is turned off, and the color fades, the elements remain hot for some time, and children — and unsuspecting adults — may not realize this and burn themselves.

Another safety consideration involves the placement of the controls. Most ranges have controls at the front of the range for convenience. These, however, can easily be reached by small children. Some ranges have controls on the side of the burners, and others have them on a raised panel at the back. The main caution with controls at the back is that you must be careful when you reach across the

---

RANGE

Features to examine
- ☐ Size: 20, 24, 30, 36, 48 inches wide
- ☐ Power source: gas, electric
- ☐ Type: free-standing, built-in, drop-in
- ☐ Gas burners: pilot light, pilotless ignition
- ☐ Electric burners: conventional coil, solid element
- ☐ Modular electric: add grill, griddle
- ☐ Ventilation system: self-vent, ducted
- ☐ If self-vent: built-in down-draft system, retractable down-draft
- ☐ Controls: rotary, push-button, touch; memory; pre-programmed delay start
- ☐ Location of controls: at front, to side of burners, on back panel
- ☐ Clock: analog, digital, timer
- ☐ Inside oven: light, food temperature probe, two or three racks
- ☐ Upper oven, if included: standard oven, microwave oven, combination microwave/convection
- ☐ Cooktop surface: baked enamel, stainless steel, glass-ceramic
- ☐ Door: without window, with window
        baked enamel, black glass, other glass (e.g. white or gray, stainless steel)
- ☐ Full or limited warranty: length of warranty, parts and labor covered

HIGH-LOW RANGE

The high-low range is so called because it has two separate ovens, one of which is lifted above the cooking surface of the lower range by a special backplate. The bottom oven is a standard size and may be self-cleaning or continuous-cleaning in operation. The top oven, though, tends to be somewhat smaller and often this oven is either a microwave or a microwave/ convection type.

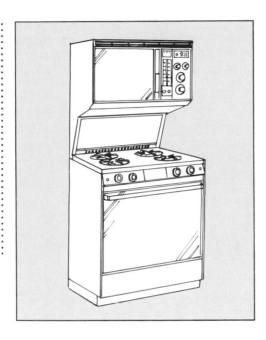

burners so that you do not inadvertently get burned by a hot pot or burner.

Some newer controls are set behind glass panels with control "pads" that are outlined to indicate temperature or timing and are activated by touch. These electronic controls can be very sophisticated, and some even have memory so that you can program in the time it will take to cook a particular food. A special preprogrammed delay start can be set so that food in the oven, or on the cooking surface, can be turned on in your absence.

The upper/lower oven — or "high-low" oven — configuration is particularly convenient if you want to use two ovens simultaneously but have no room for an entire wall oven or two. Many ranges offer a microwave oven or a combination microwave/convection oven in this position. One caution: Be sure that you can reach into an upper oven without straining your back. Also, be sure that burners are off, or covered, when you pull foods out of the

upper oven. You could burn yourself, and, of course, small children should not use an upper oven for the same reason.

Materials will dictate your stylistic choice, and the newest of these is glass-ceramic, in black or white. Black glass has been popular for a number of years; white glass and gray glass are new entries into the market. Many professional cooks like stainless steel; some combine styles. For example, the cooking surface may be stainless, but the door may be black glass. If you are a traditionalist, baked enamel is still available; white is the most popular choice.

COMMERCIAL GAS RANGE

Commercial gas ranges, those stainless steel behemoths favored by restaurateurs, became a status symbol of the 1970s in homes, and they continue to be popular today. True, the capacity of these giants is tremendous, but many homeowners, dazzled by their glamorous image, did not take into consideration just how these ranges function most efficiently, namely, at full capacity and all day long. Pros, in fact, heat up the range and keep it heated and in continuous use throughout a long work day.

Commercial ranges must be installed correctly because of the gas connections and because they radiate a great deal of heat. Much like wood stoves, they must be set at a certain distance from the wall, and both walls and floor must be sheathed with a fire-resistant and heat-proof substance, such as tile. Because the commercial range is so heavy, be certain that your floor can support the extra weight. Because it radiates considerable heat, the commercial range should remain free-standing; it should not be set in between cabinets unless proper insulation is inserted on either side of the appliance.

There are new, smaller commercial-style

COMMERCIAL GAS RANGE

**Favored by restaurants
because of its vast capacity
for cooking in quantity
and for its maintenance of
an even heat over the long
day, the commercial gas
range is a popular choice
among gourmet cooks, or
those inclined to enter-
taining. Bulky and heavy,
though, this appliance
requires extra support
under the floor and also
extra insulation all around.
The range must be set away
from the wall to protect the
wall from its intense heat.**

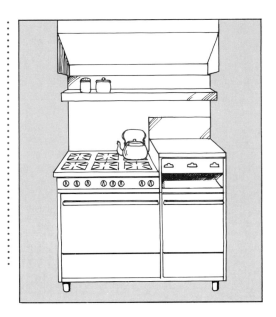

gives off a more even and consistent heat, and they dislike having to bend down to pull out foods from the oven, especially heavy foods such as a giant turkey.

The solution: Separate the cooktop from the oven, and set the oven — or pair of ovens — higher in a wall cabinet. Wall ovens today are a popular option.

Wall ovens may be chosen in a variety of configurations. A single oven can be used alone or to supplement a full-feature range nearby. Twin ovens can stack. The ovens can be twins, with both operating in exactly the same way. Or one oven may have a self-cleaning option while the other must be cleaned in the old-fashioned way, with oven cleaner and elbow grease! The top oven may be a microwave oven or an oven with a microwave/convection option in addition to its standard cooking ability.

Controls for both ovens, if both are standard, are typically placed at eye level. Controls, as on the range, may be rotary, push-button, or touch. The electronic controls, again, are more sophisticated. Because microwave cooking is so fast, a microwave oven will have independent controls.

Black glass seems to be the material of choice, probably because transparent black glass can act as a window when the oven light is turned on. Opaque glass will have a window insert.

Wall ovens come in three widths: 24, 27, and 30 inches (27 is the norm).

Some homeowners who still want to separate the cooktop from the oven — but who do not have extra space — are placing their wall oven (or a pair) beneath the countertop, in place of one or two base cabinets. And sometimes, too, they will place a single wall oven under an independent cooktop! If you would like to try out this particular combination, be certain there is enough room for venting the oven.

Wall ovens usually come with removable doors; this is especially handy when you must

ranges now available, however, and these have been developed for residential use. They have a similar appearance, but they do not need to be cooked on — or in — continuously to function at maximum efficiency. They operate much as a standard range would.

Before purchasing a commercial gas range, ask yourself:

Do you cook often?
Do you cook in quantity?
Do you cook often for large parties?
Would you use other features, such as the grill or the griddle, as well as the burners and the ovens, often? Is the higher expense of a commercial range worth it?

ELECTRIC WALL OVEN

Those who have owned ranges have two major grievances: one, the position of the oven, and two, the power source. Many gas range owners long for an electric oven that

ing. In a microwave oven, microwaves, powered by electricity, travel in straight trajectories through the oven, bouncing from wall to wall. They cause the molecules in food to agitate, thus cooking the food. Microwaves cook food from the inside out; portions of the food may remain cool or uncooked, and so most microwave ovens come with turntables that revolve foods during the cooking cycle.

SINGLE WALL OVEN AND DOUBLE WALL OVEN

Many homeowners who plan on separating their cooktop from their ovens opt to stack a pair of wall ovens out of the line of traffic and out of the work triangle. A single wall oven is a perfectly suitable solution for a family that does not do a great deal of oven cookery, though. With both a single or a double oven, the controls should be set at eye level; the controls will be easier to read and easy to reach, too.

pull an exceedingly heavy item from the oven. If you are transferring baked goods, such as cookies, to a rack on the countertop, this feature is very convenient.

When planning the surrounding cabinetry for stacking ovens, note that, together, twin units stretch 50 inches in height. Also, ovens may be 24 inches deep but require room at the back for venting. Because wall ovens are usually positioned for easy reach, you will have lots of room underneath for extra storage.

MICROWAVE OVEN

One of the greatest conveniences to come into the kitchen in recent years is the microwave oven. Almost half of the households in this country, says an NAHB study, want a microwave as a second oven.

Microwaving is a much faster form of cook-

CONVECTION COOKING

Convection cooking circulates hot air at great speeds around foods to be baked or roasted. Convection cooking works up to one-third times faster than conventional baking or roasting. In addition, you can transfer frozen meats directly to a convection oven without thawing.

Because foods brown so nicely by convection, adding the right crispness, convection is often combined with microwave — in the same appliance. The microwave setting is used first, to cook the food throughout, and then the oven can be switched to the convection mode to crisp or brown the outside of the food.

The circulating air allows for quantity baking. You can use three racks rather than just two.

Convection cooking does not work well for moist foods such as stews or casseroles; save your microwave mode for these foods.

Convection and microwave cooking are cool, so ovens that operate on these modes — but not as a supplemental system to a conventional cooking mode — will not need venting.

MICROWAVE OVEN

Microwaves, large or small and free-standing or built-in, are the most sought-after appliances on the market today. If the micro-wave is to be built in, it is usually placed over the range—to consolidate cooking functions in one activity center. Countertop models can be moved any-where: If you use a micro-wave only to defrost foods, you may want to keep it near the refrigerator, and if you use it to heat up snacks, you may want to set it out on a counter near the eating center.

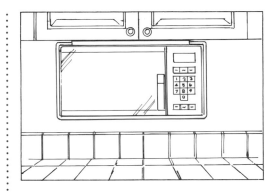

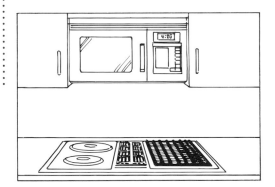

Because microwave cooking is so fast, the food must be constantly monitored. Stirring, rotating, and probing directives are written into recipes to insure even cooking.

Microwaving is very convenient for thawing out frozen foods, for reheating leftovers, and for doing such tricks as heating coffee in a matter of seconds or baking a potato in less than 6 minutes. The cooking of food multiplies geometrically; if one potato is joined by three others, for example, it will take 24 minutes to cook all four.

Microwaves vary enormously in size these days. And they vary in how they are installed. Smaller models, designed to be placed directly on the countertop or hung under a cabinet, will only take single servings, not a whole turkey. Microwaves that can be installed under the cabinet should come with their own mounting kits. The smallest microwaves measure just 13 inches by 13 inches by 12 inches deep. The largest are equal in size to a wall oven; in fact, the largest *are* wall oven models. Countertop models can be as wide as 33 inches but are not as tall as the wall oven version. Large countertop models may be matched in capacity by wall oven models.

A microwave oven can be set over the range so that it looks built into the cabinet run over-head. An installation kit comes with this type of microwave so that you can lock the oven in under the cabinet; be sure to specify that you will be doing this so that the cabinet that will anchor the oven will be the appropriate size, both in width and height. The overhead cabinet usually measures 30 inches wide to comple-ment the standard range below; be sure the microwave you choose is the same width. If, however, you choose a range that is narrower or wider than the standard, you should make certain that the microwave and the overhead cabinet match up.

Where you position your microwave is, of course, up to you. Check to see if the door opens to the right or to the left; in some cases it may fold down. You will want the door to open so that you can remove foods easily to a nearby counter. Controls can be simple, based on timing by the minute, up to, say, 15 minutes, or they can be quite complex, with directions and times for particular foods indicated right on separate electronic touch pads on the face of the machine. The most sophisticated models have several heat set-tings, and they will have automatic food tem-perature probes set inside the oven cavity as well. Check, too, for a special "defrost" set-ting and for a "temperature hold" setting that will maintain food at a warm temperature until you are ready to serve. Because microwaving works best for moist foods, foods that you would like to bake or roast would not be prepared in the microwave. However, with combination convection/microwave capabilities now available, this problem has been overcome in some of the newer ovens. When the microwave or microwave/convection mode is part of a standard oven, the oven will probably have a self-cleaning feature as well. Some microwaves are so versatile that they will switch over to a toaster/broiler mode, or back into a standard radiant mode, just like a regular oven.

Features to check for include a turntable, to keep the food rotating during the cooking cycle, and a timer that also indicates the time of day. Digital displays count down the cooking action in minutes and seconds. And a temperature probe will react to overcooking.

Until recently many people were hesitant about using microwave ovens because of the "radiation" of waves. Microwave ovens are constructed under rigorous codes and restrictions and all come with a mandatory safety feature that turns the oven off immediately when the door is not latched tight. To be safe, though, always follow microwave instructions exactly, and be sure to train all members of your household how to use the appliance.

Follow microwave recipes carefully, too.

Microwaving requires special utensils. No metals can be used, as the microwaves bounce off of them and can severely damage the oven. There are many microwave-safe utensils available in stores today. Paper, glass, and china can also be used. The utensil never heats up as much as the food.

ELECTRIC COOKTOP

Electric cooktops come in four modes: conventional electric coil; solid element, also called "disc"; glass-ceramic smoothtop; and induction smoothtop.

Conventional Electrical Coil Cooktop

This is the traditional type and still the most commonly chosen cooktop. The standard cooktop provides four burners, two larger and two smaller coils, with controls set either beside the burners or between them at the front of the burner. Heat travels by conduction from the radiant coil into the utensil and into the food. One disadvantage to the electric coil is that it returns to its original hue soon after the power is turned off but remains hot. This can be dangerous, especially to young children who may not know the coil is still too hot to touch. Check to see that the burners are removable, and that they have drip pans that can be removed, too, for easy cleaning. The cooktop comes in baked enamel or stainless steel.

Solid Element Cooktop

Like the coil type, the solid element cooktop has a standard set of four elements or discs, two larger and two smaller, with controls placed beside or between them. The solid element, or disc, is made of cast-iron. The electrical elements embedded in the insulated discs

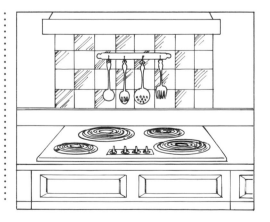

ELECTRIC COIL COOKTOP

The traditional electric cooktop transmits heat through electric coils. The most common configuration pairs two large burners behind two smaller ones, or one large and one small front and back. It is most efficient to use the coil that matches up with the base of your cooking utensil so that you do not waste energy.

SOLID ELEMENT COOKTOP

The disc-type cooktop has been used in Europe for a number of years and is now being either imported or widely copied in the U.S. The cast-iron discs transfer heat more evenly than the standard electric coil and are easier to keep clean as well.

GLASS-CERAMIC COOKTOP

The flat and smooth surface of the glass-ceramic cooktop is sleek to look at and easy to wipe clean. It can be difficult, however, to ascertain when or whether a particular area of the cooking surface is hot. Look closely at the outlines where pots are to be placed to see if they have changed color—this indicates how hot the cooking area actually is. Utensils with a perfectly flat base work best as they assure an even distribution of heat to the food within the utensil.

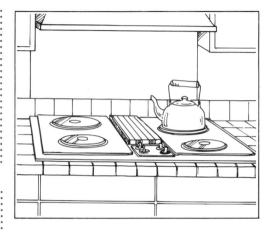

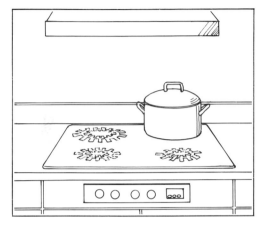

transfer the heat by conduction from the disc into the pot and to the food. The disc is preferred by many cooks because heat is evenly distributed over the surface of the disc, whereas heat is not evenly transmitted around the standard coil. Some discs are made with thermal sensors that register heat control; these sensors, centered on the discs, change color so that you know when the power is on or off. A small child, however, might not be able to distinguish whether or not the disc is on. The surface of the solid element cooktop can be found in stainless steel, in a baked enamel finish, and in black, white, or gray glass-ceramic. Some solid element cooktops are thermostatically controlled.

Glass-Ceramic Cooktop

This type of cooktop operates in the same manner as the conventional coil, for coils do indeed heat this cooktop, but they are set underneath a slick glass ceramic plate that is totally smooth. The areas that heat up are indicated on the glass by circles, sunbursts, or other outlines; these change color when the area is heated. Again, the danger lies in not realizing that a portion of the cooktop is

hot. When glass-ceramic cooktops were first introduced years ago, they were all white; these were discontinued. New versions of this type of cooktop are made of black glass-ceramic material. The main advantage of this type of cooktop is that it will wipe clean easily as there are no ridges on the surface in which to catch grease or food.

Induction Cooktop

The surface of this type of smooth cooktop is identical to the glass-ceramic cooktop, but the power and cooking function is entirely different. Solid-state elements under the smooth surface generate a magnetic field which, in turn, induces a current within a ferromagnetic utensil set on the surface. The current causes the molecules in the food inside the utensil to agitate, thus cooking the food. Because of this magnetic action the cooktop stays cool during the entire process. Many cooks prefer the induction cooktop for its precise control. Fractional heat settings are possible; even melting chocolate is an easy task, with little risk of burning. The types of cooking utensils that can be used with the induction cooktop include cast-iron or carbon-steel (these are ferromagnetic); however, other

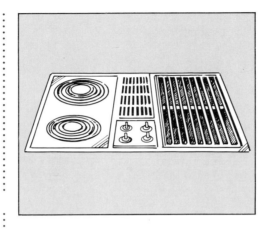

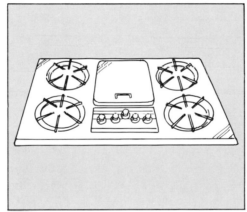

metals, such as copper and aluminum, which do not have a magnetic attraction, will not work. Induction cooktops are still costly because of their solid-state circuitry.

Convertible Cooktop

Certain electric cooktops will incorporate all of the previously discussed types of cooktops into their design, as pop-in cartridges that slide into receptacles in the central unit. The smallest convertible cooktop has one receptacle; the standard has two; and the largest has three, usually with a special down-draft

ventilation system incorporated into the configuration between two of the receptacles. The various cartridges pop in and out very easily. Each of the cooking cartridges has two burners. Other cartridges may include a grill element and a griddle. Accessories, such as a kabob-rotisserie, a deep fryer, and a wok are also very popular.

GAS COOKTOP

Gas cooktops, favored by professional cooks, can be obtained in both a residential and a restaurant gauge. Pros consider the accuracy of control vital — the flame on a gas cooktop can be fine-tuned in infinitesimal increments to insure precise cooking. Although most come in a standard four-burner configuration, there are gas cooktops available with six and even eight burners. Some kitchen designers like to purchase single burners to position in a row; they prefer to keep pots side by side, to avoid reaching over one to get to another at the back of the cooktop. Gas cooktops are typically crafted of stainless steel with porcelain-clad, cast-iron burners. A baked enamel finish is also available; a handsome version is all black.

GAS WALL OVEN

Recently gas wall ovens have become available for those who prefer to roast or bake by gas. Features are similar to electrics and include the same types of controls, timer and clock, light, removable oven doors, and self-cleaning option. An electrical hookup is required for "pilotless" ignition.

GAS-FIRED BARBECUE

Those who love grilling outdoors may want to include a barbecue unit in the kitchen. In a gas-fired barbecue, gas heats lava rocks under a cast-iron grill. These barbecues must be installed with a suitable ventilating hood directly overhead to waft away odors and fumes. The hibachi, another outdoor favorite, is not recommended for indoor use because charcoals emit toxic fumes.

EXHAUST HOOD

Cooking releases smoke, grease, moisture, steam, odors, and heat into the air, and so the cooktop and/or the range should be vented to the outside of the house. For this reason, it is wise to place the cooking appliance on an outside wall of your house or apartment to minimize the distance the ventilating duct will have to run. If you prefer to situate your cooktop on a peninsula or island, the ventilating duct will have to run a greater distance.

Some cooktops and ranges come with a built-in, down-draft ventilating system. This type of system runs beneath the cabinet or island and floor to the outside and liberates the space over the cooktop or range to be used for other purposes, such as a pot rack hung from the ceiling.

A ducted hood can be installed from the ceiling or mounted onto the wall. Wall-mounted hoods tend to be more compact than ceiling hoods. You should, though, select a hood that is as wide as your cooktop; an extension of 6 inches all around looks better visually, and this extension is usually accomplished by a simple flare in the design.

The strength and efficiency of the fan located inside the hood dictates how effective it will be in removing offensive odors and such. An effective hood fan should change the air in the kitchen once every 4 minutes. This is measured in cubic feet of air per minute or CFMs. Every linear foot of hood should have between 100 and 120 CFMs.

CHECKLIST FOR IMPORTED APPLIANCES

☐ Is the extra cost, which can be substantial, worth it?
☐ If electric, is it approved by the Underwriters Laboratories? Does it have the UL seal?
☐ If gas, is it approved by the American Gas Association?
☐ Will there be an unreasonable delay in delivery? Is it back-ordered?
☐ Can the appliance be serviced easily and conveniently?
☐ Are replacement parts readily available or would they have to be imported in response to your request?
☐ If the appliance is a range, does it self-clean? And if it is a refrigerator or freezer, is it no-frost?

The fan usually operates at different speeds to accelerate removal of odors and the like. Most hoods, too, incorporate a light into the unit.

Both air change and noise level are rated by the Home Ventilating Institute; check ratings on the label of the unit you are considering purchasing.

Top-of-the-line ventilating hoods will offer infinite speed control and a memory so that you can program the speed at which smoke and odors from particular foods are drawn from the room. A special warning system built into the best hoods will automatically turn the blower to a higher speed if there is excess heat. The built-in light can be brightened or dimmed; on the dimmer setting this light can function as an ambient light when other overhead lighting in the kitchen is turned off.

**WALL-MOUNTED
EXHAUST HOOD**

**WALL-MOUNTED
EXHAUST HOOD**

The wall-mounted hood may come in one of two versions. The first, a small unit, merely filters grease, fumes, and odors, and must be cleaned often. The second, a more efficient type, ventilates to the outdoors, thus assuring removal of grease, odors, smoke, fumes, and moisture from the room. The ventilated hood keeps your kitchen cleaner as these noxious dirt-inducing agents will be minimized. For maximum efficiency the hood should be set about 5 feet off the floor; it should also be inset slightly to give you adequate headroom when you work at the cooking center.

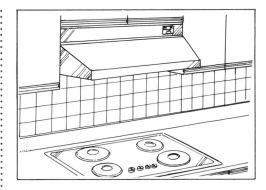

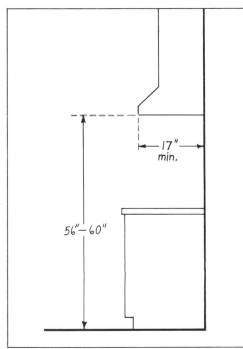

A hood should be installed so that it will not obstruct your view of the cooking surface; you don't want to bump your head into the unit either. The standard distance is from 56 inches to 60 inches off the floor.

Ductless hoods are not recommended because grease builds up inside the unit; this can be a fire hazard. Ductless hoods cannot remove odors, moisture, or heat. Many high-low ranges — those with an oven over the range — come with ductless hoods; be sure to install another ventilating device in the kitchen to remove odors, moisture, and heat. Installing a ceiling fan or window fan is a particularly good solution. Remember, too, to clean the grease out of the hood filter often. Wall ovens should have built-in exhaust fans.

REFRIGERATOR/FREEZER

The refrigerator/freezer is gradually slimming down without losing any of its precious interior capacity for food storage. The average refrigerator/freezer still protrudes beyond the standard cabinet depth, but more manufacturers are designing units that reposition or minimize the compressor so that the appliance can, indeed, be slipped right in between cabinets in perfect alignment.

The most common refrigerator/freezer configuration, the top-mount freezer type, varies in capacity from about 14 cubic feet to 32 cubic feet.

Refrigerators, both standard door and side-by-side models, measure from 24 to 60 inches in width and from 58 inches to 72 inches in height. Be sure to leave an inch above the refrigerator for ventilation.

Refrigerators come with a leveling adjustment at the base of the appliance; the device will elevate any corner of the refrigerator by up to 2 inches.

To calculate how big your appliance should be, figure on about 10 cubic feet for each of the first two people in your household, and then add an additional cubic foot per person. If you hoard foods or entertain often, up this figure another cubic foot or two.

STANDARD TOP-MOUNT REFRIGERATOR/FREEZER

The top-mount refrigerator/ freezer is the most common of all refrigerator types and is selected most often because the convenience of storing frozen foods, and especially ice, at eye level is enormously appealing to many people. Deep pockets on the doors allow for storage of bulky items such as half-gallons and gallons of milk, juice, and soda. Doors on the top-mount can be opened either to the left or to the right; the door should open toward the adjacent counter.

The side-by-side configuration is more convenient for many families, especially those with small children, who find reaching into a top-mount freezer compartment awkward. Side-by-sides, although they have an overall capacity that is large — up to 27 cubic feet — are, in fact, quite narrow and deep in each section, so you have to plan your storage carefully for easy access.

Top-of-the-line refrigerator/freezers in both the top-mount and side-by-side versions sport all sorts of added attractions. Through-the-door ice and chilled water dispensers are handy, as are so-called "entertainment centers," which are like mini-bars set right into the door. You pull down a door, which becomes a shelf, and snacks and beverages can be stored inside the cubby. Electronic monitors in some models indicate equivalent temperatures in the refrigerator and in the freezer and warn if the temperature falls to a point that could

SIDE-BY-SIDE REFRIGERATOR/FREEZER

The side-by-side is a winning combination because you can keep most-used or replaced foods in either compartment at eye level, and bulkier or less urgently needed foods below. The most luxurious models of the side-by-side offer an ''entertainment center'' insert which can be opened without opening the door of the refrigerator itself. Other built-ins include an ice maker that dispenses ice through the door and a chilled water dispenser.

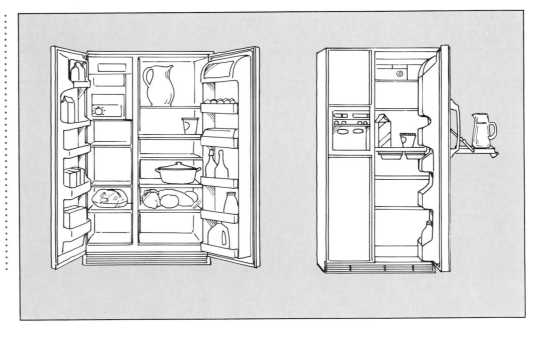

**FRENCH-DOOR
REFRIGERATOR WITH
PULLOUT FREEZER**

The so-called French door refrigerator is an increasingly popular take on the side-by-side refrigerator because the huge freezer drawer functions almost like a separate chest-style freezer. Its capacity is great enough to accommodate even the largest turkey.

**BOTTOM-MOUNT
REFRIGERATOR/FREEZER**

The bottom-mount version of the refrigerator/freezer simply swaps the freezer and the refrigerator compartments. If you freeze foods over the long term and don't, in fact, go into the freezer all that often, the bottom-mount may prove more convenient for you.

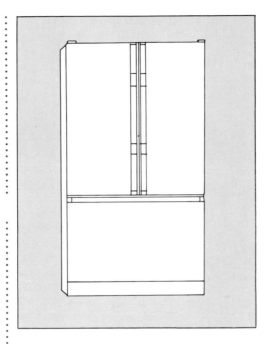

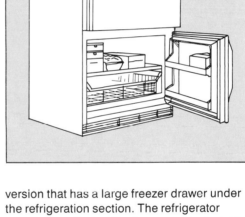

encourage spoilage of perishables. A clock/timer may be featured, too.

In-freezer options include an ice maker; some of these can double their yield at the touch of a lever. An ice-cream maker and a yogurt maker are two other freezer inserts available in some models.

Virtually standard in all models are adjustable shelves and bins, egg cartons, and ice trays. Some models have trays that slide in under shelves and then transfer to the microwave oven. A wine storage caddy may slot in on one side of the refrigerator. In the doors, deeper bins accommodate gallon-size containers and very tall bottles.

Bottom-mount refrigerator/freezers are gaining in popularity. The basic bottom-mount simply reverses the refrigerator and the freezer, with the freezer on the bottom. The freezer itself is outfitted with bins and shelves that pull out for easy access. An alternative is the

version that has a large freezer drawer under the refrigeration section. The refrigerator opens normally, but the freezer pulls straight out underneath. A third version is the so-called "French-door" model. In this version the refrigerator sports side-by-side doors, and the freezer, again, is a large pull-out drawer.

The newest refrigerators and freezers that are being imported from Europe and marketed under American auspices are modular. The smaller refrigerator and freezer components measure just under 24 inches wide and deep and 34½ inches high so that they can slide in under a countertop. But these can also stack, allowing you to decide whether the refrigerator or the freezer should be on top.

The taller components stand 78 inches high; these, again, are about 24 inches wide and deep. They may stand alone or in tandem. Or, you may decide you need two refrigerators and one freezer or vice versa.

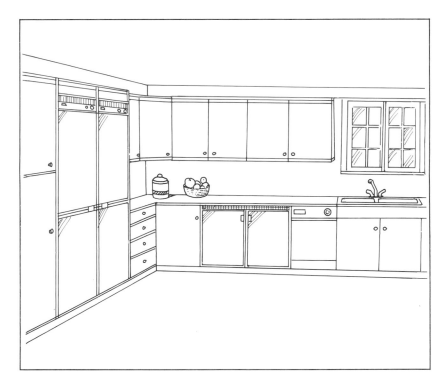

MODULAR REFRIGERATOR/FREEZER

Another European import, the modular refrigerator/ freezer combination allows you to choose just how many refrigerator or freezer units you want, and how big you want them to be. You can add an extra module to a basic refrigerator and freezer lineup if you like. You can stack modules or place them side-by-side. It's up to you and your specific needs.

All of the new components run flush to the front of the cabinetry for a clean look, and they come with trim kits so that you can add panels to match your cabinets exactly.

Compact refrigerators and freezers may tuck in under counters, and the tiniest types sit on top of a counter. The smallest of these offer between 2 and 5 cubic feet of space, but door bins are usually deep enough to accommodate large bottles.

Be sure to specify a left- or a right-hand opening in the standard-door version. You want to be able to open the refrigerator and freezer doors toward the nearest counter, especially if the appliance is located at the end of a cabinet run.

Styling is similar to other appliances. You can choose among several enamel colors or black glass or trim kits to accommodate panels to match your cabinetry.

Virtually all refrigerator/freezers are no-frost except the least expensive single-door models.

If you entertain a great deal, consider adding a separate ice maker to your appliance lineup. This can be installed under the countertop wherever it is most convenient; many people place it near the bar sink because it does need a plumbing hookup.

CHEST FREEZER

If you store enormous quantities of foods, such as sides of beef and harvested vegetables, a chest freezer is a must. The chest freezer, however, usually resides in the basement or mudroom or pantry, out of the way of the kitchen itself but within easy access.

Sizes of freezers vary from a little over 5 cubic feet to double that capacity. Measurements run from 23½ inches to 31 inches to 42⅛ inches wide. Heights change only slightly, from 35 inches to almost 36 inches and, with the lid up, from 55 inches to 56½ inches.

Look for a temperature monitor on the freezer and for a drain at the front of the freezer to aid in defrosting.

SINK

The sink has become the latest glamour item in the kitchen. Even in an old, staid kitchen layout, the simple change of a sink with high-style companion faucets and accessories can add a touch of sophistication to the overall look of the room.

Traditionally, the sink was considered an indispensable item but hardly a designer's dream. European imports have changed that notion. Sleek shapes from Europe, including rounds and ovals, as well as clean-lined fittings and accessories, are increasing in popularity.

CHEST FREEZER

The chest freezer is an old standby, but one that is still necessary to many households where storing quantities of food over the long term is mandatory. The chest freezer is usually placed in a garage or a pantry or a basement— out of the flow of traffic.

KITCHEN SINK

You probably spend more time at the sink than at any other appliance in the kitchen. Once the choice of a sink was merely a choice of one bowl or two. Triple-bowl sinks are commonplace now, and the newest European models are round instead of curve-corner rectangles. Inserts such as drying bins and cutting boards are common, too. An optional, integral drain board extends the wet surface to one side of the sink. Sinks may be crafted of stainless steel or porcelain over cast-iron.

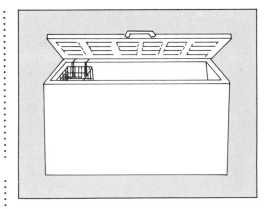

In practical terms, the sink may be purchased in a single-bowl, double-bowl, or triple-bowl configuration. Sizes of each bowl vary, but basic depths are 6, 8, or 10 inches. The largest sink — with three bowls plus drain board — runs 60 inches wide. The center bowl in this version is a small, shallow inset, handy for rinsing flatware or small items.

Stainless steel is the preferred choice of many consumers, but enamel-over-cast-iron runs a close second, and many colors are available in this finish. Stainless steel sinks may have a built-in drain board on one side. Both types of sinks have a raised lip all around to prevent spills over the edge. Choose the 18-gauge weight in stainless steel; it is stronger than the 20-gauge.

Most sinks come with a self-rim. Some, however, are designed to be recessed under the cut-out, and some slip in so that the sides are flush with the edge of the cut-out. Check to be sure how your sink must be fit into the countertop, and specify accordingly.

Accessory inserts include such items as a cutting board, a colander, a drain bowl, and a cutlery bin.

Faucets and fittings vary widely. A single-lever faucet is a common and useful choice. The rising faucet pulls up to 10 inches in height

FAUCETS

The faucet you choose will aid in washing and rinsing both dinnerware and larger pots and pans. The high-arc faucet usually used at the bar sink is a good alternative to the standard faucet if you will be washing many large items. The single-lever faucet controls both hot and cold water through the single unit. The two-handle faucet requires three predrilled holes in the sink.

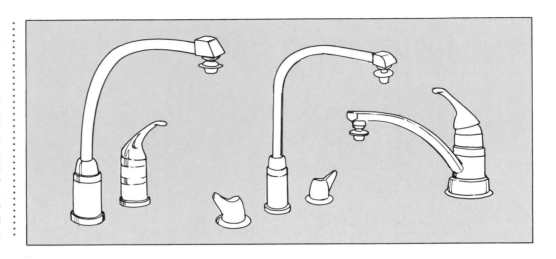

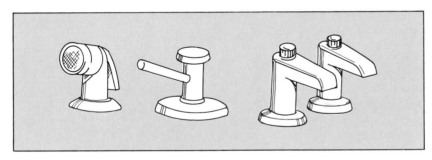

ACCESSORIES

The sink can accept an array of accessories besides the faucet. The retractable spray hose eases rinsing. The soap lotion dispenser can be used for liquid soap or for hand lotion; if you want both, you can have two installed. The instant hot water dispenser comes in handy for instant coffee, tea, or soup, and the chilled water dispenser is also a nice addition.

to accommodate large pots or vases underneath the running water. The high-arc faucet, usually installed in bar sinks, is another option. Add-ons include a hot water dispenser, a soap dispenser, a spray unit on a flexible hose, and a water purifier for drinking water. Faucets and fittings may be metal, usually stainless steel or brass, or they may come in bright enamel colors as well. The most technologically advanced faucets exhibit electronic readouts that indicate water temperature variations as the water is running.

Once you have decided which fittings you want for your sink, be sure to specify these when you order. Sinks are always predrilled to conform to the configuration that is chosen; you cannot drill in extra holes afterwards; therefore, if you want several dispensers in addition to your faucet, say so before you buy.

When you install any sink, it is wise to position it as close to the front edge of its base cabinet as possible; this relieves the back strain caused by leaning forward too far over a sink. Consider, too, an off-center drain in one bowl of the sink if you will be adding a garbage disposal. This will leave more room free under the sink for storage.

DISHWASHER

Most dishwashers are standardized; they measure 24 inches wide and deep by 34 inches high so that they will fit in under a countertop. You can specify a different surface if you wish; some manufacturers offer butcher block on top of the appliance. The newest dishwasher models, for the sake of space in small dwellings, slip in under the sink. Such a dishwasher, although it will easily hook up to existing plumbing, requires a sink that is shallower than the norm. Ask your appliance salesperson

DISHWASHER

The dishwasher has liberated the homeowner from many of the most tedious tasks in the kitchen. Nowadays the dishwasher can seemingly perform miracles; different settings can be pushed for fine crystal or china or for seriously soiled pots and pans. The energy-saving mode dries dishes without heat.

to specify the correct sink that will complement this dishwasher.

Even the most basic dishwashers differentiate between light and heavy wash loads; more sophisticated models have settings for fine crystal and china and others for heavily soiled pots and pans. A rinse and hold feature for rinsing and storing small loads until the dishwasher is full is commonplace. The energy-saving option aerates dishes to dry them without heat.

Check to see if the appliance has a self-cleaning filter and check the spray arm, too. This arm should rotate swiftly in a full orbit to disperse water evenly throughout the cavity, or tub, in the machine. The racks in the tub should be flexible enough to accommodate tall glasses and large pots and pans. Some racks remove and shift around for various types of loads.

The most sensitive controls monitor water temperature to assure best results in any washing cycle. This monitor beeps or flashes to warn of problems with drainage or a power failure. Noise can be a problem with dishwashers, so be sure that the appliance is well insulated for a quiet run.

Many dishwashers can be purchased with separate panels that can be fitted on the sides. Front panels, as for other appliances, can be fitted to match any cabinetry. Black glass and enamel are two design options.

TRASH COMPACTOR

The disposal of bulky garbage and trash is one thankless chore that has been made much easier thanks to the convenience of the trash compactor. The compactor compresses trash and garbage under extreme pressure — between 2,300 and 3,500 pounds of force — to a fraction of its bulk. In fact, the normal trash generated by a family of four should pack into one weekly bag; one bag of compacted trash weighs about 20 to 25 pounds. Some compactors require special lined waste bags that are sold to fit those models; other compactors, though, accept standard grocery bags. The compactor should have an inner bag caddy with handles for lifting out the heavy bag.

The bag fits into a drawer that slides or tilts out from the body of the machine. To open the drawer, one must step on a foot pedal or lift a handle on the drawer itself. The foot pedal was devised for convenience: A person holding garbage may have difficulty manipulating a handle. Some compactors come with a pedal and a handle.

The trash compactor you select should be heavily insulated for sound absorption and it should include an "anti-jam" device so that trash won't lock the crushing mechanism

TRASH COMPACTOR

The trash compactor, which can be pulled around in the rollaway model or installed under the counter, compresses trash and garbage to a fraction of its accumulated volume. When the compactor is built in, it is usually installed between the food preparation area and the sink—logical since most garbage builds up in these two areas.

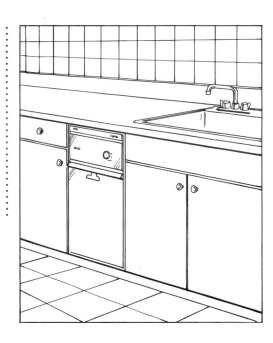

and damage the machine. Look, too, for a compartment that holds an air freshener.

Trash compactors measure 12 inches, 15 inches, and sometimes 18 inches wide and are usually installed under the counter near the sink. Free-standing units, which roll on casters, are also available. The front of the compactor is outfitted with a panel, often reversible, so that you can match it to your

other appliances, or with the surrounding cabinetry.

GARBAGE DISPOSAL

The garbage disposal or food waste disposer — or "pig" — is easily hooked up to the drain under your sink, and it will grind up certain foods before releasing them, under water pressure, into your waste pipe. Soft foods, eggshells, coffee grounds, and the like can be ground and washed away; hard foods, such as bones, should not be fed to the disposal.

The "grinding chamber," or food waste cavity, should be constructed of a noncorrosive material. The lid serves to lock the food in. Some lids turn the machine on with a quick twist. Safer, though, is the lid that locks with a separate switch to turn the disposal on and off. Look for an overload protection switch; you switch this on if too much food slows down the grinding action of the machine. Many areas of the country, especially some larger cities, do not permit the installation of disposals because they do not want to release food waste into the city pipes. Some areas of the country, on the other hand, require disposals because they cut down on bagged garbage that would otherwise go to the dump. Be sure to check your local building code before installing a disposal in your kitchen.

5 STORAGE

No one ever has enough storage space, especially in the kitchen. Planning for the perfect amount of storage, then, may be a Herculean feat. But planning can be a real pleasure; the key is to calculate just how much space you need to fit everything you now own, and then to add in enough extra space so that you can spread out your belongings while leaving room for new acquisitions.

Do you really need everything you own right now, though? Are there items that take up a great deal of space that you rarely, if ever, use? Can you get rid of some of these things without offending anyone?

CALCULATING YOUR NEEDS

The minimum amount of space set out by a National Home Builders study guideline recommends that you have at least 72 running inches of cabinetry — based on base cabinets with a run of wall cabinets overhead. One hundred and twenty inches is more liberal, but allowing more than that will add to the steps you have to take to find something you may urgently need and may overwhelm the work triangle, too.

The easiest way to calculate your needs is to take everything you have in your kitchen — especially the dinnerware and the kitchenware — and set it all out on the floor in piles and stacks. See how much room each stack takes up. Place stacks of similar items near each other and mentally visualize "shelves" for each group of items. Rearrange stacks until you find comfortable groupings and make lists or diagrams of each "shelf-load" and where it will go.

When you think about placing items in cabinets, be sure to put most-used items at an easy-to-reach level, somewhere between your shoulders and your eyes in a wall cabinet and just at knee level or above in a base cabinet. Place less-used items high up or low down. Don't place heavy items too high because they can be dangerous to remove.

It makes sense to locate items near the activity center where they will be most used. And label each shelf so that every member of your family can help clean up and replace items after use.

Caution: In households with young children or pets, never store household cleaning agents or other poisonous materials under the sink.

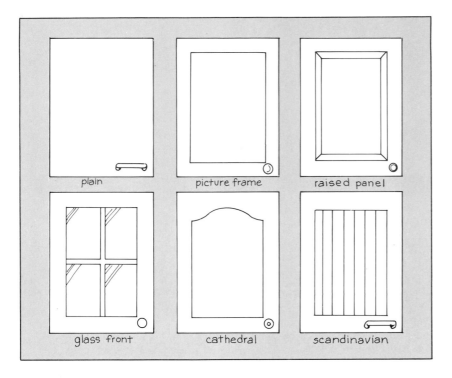

plain

picture frame

raised panel

glass front

cathedral

scandinavian

CABINET DOOR STYLES

Along with the finish, the door style will dictate the look of your cabinetry. Some styles appear rustic while others exhibit a more contemporary flair. You can replace the doors on existing cabinets, too, if you want to change their look without changing or dismantling the entire unit.

Keep them near the sink but up out of the reach of children. And place child-proof locks on all base cabinets. Many mothers reserve one base cabinet for kitchen items that a child can play with without danger; lightweight pots and spoons, for example, can be kept in this location — just for fun.

CHOOSING CABINETS

The cabinets in your kitchen fill the most space; because of their visibility, they quickly establish the design look in the room and are the clearest indicator of your kitchen's "personality." Cabinets may be built to order by a cabinetmaker or carpenter, or they may be purchased as "stock" items and then assembled in line-ups to conform to the specific kitchen plan you have chosen. Knock-down, unassembled cabinets, which come flat in cartons, can be put together in the room.

Kitchen cabinets run the gamut, in terms of design, from sleek contemporary to cozy country. The hardware you choose adds to the visual appeal, too. Cabinets may be built of solid wood or they may be made of a core material, such as plywood or particleboard, which is then veneered with laminate to simulate any material. Plastic laminates come in a vast array of colors and textures; some textures are so close to the "original," be it wood or steel or another material, that it is difficult to tell the difference!

Basically, cabinets conform to a modular system. The narrowest are 9 inches wide, and they increase in 3-inch increments up to 48 inches wide. Cabinets under 24 inches wide come with a single door and you have to specify a right- or a left-hand opening; cabinets over 24 inches wide have double doors.

Each appliance requires a cabinet surround of a specific depth, width, and height. Measure your appliances before selecting the cabinets that may enclose them, and then ascertain which cabinets will work best. The cabinets that go between can then be measured to fit precisely.

Remember: Dark woods and dark colors make a room appear smaller and cozier; light tones, light colors, and white will visually expand the space.

Once you have figured out your cabinet needs, you must decide whether you want the cabinets custom-made or if they can be fitted together from stock sizes. Check your local kitchen dealer for your options; kitchen dealers supervise installation of stock cabinets that they sell.

BASE CABINETS

Base cabinets measure 30½ inches high and 24 inches deep. Their widths vary, from

BASE CABINETS

Ready-made cabinets are standardized, increasing in 3-inch increments from 9 inches on up to 48 inches. To create wider cabinets, two or more smaller cabinets are combined to achieve a unified look. If you want a totally uniform design, you can have cabinets custom-tailored to your exact measurements by a cabinetmaker knowledgeable about kitchen design.

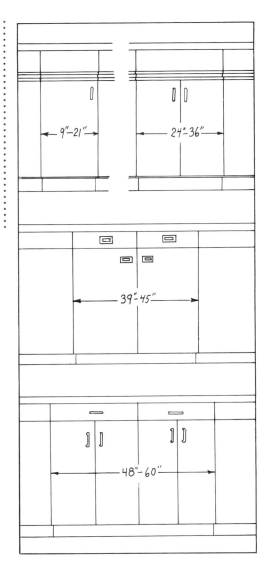

CABINET CHECKLIST

☐ How is the cabinet constructed? Does it seem strong and sturdy?

☐ Are the hinges on the doors visible or are they concealed?

☐ Is the interior of the cabinet finished so that it matches the exterior or front of the cabinet?

☐ Does the cabinet have a strong, finished back?

☐ How many shelves, if any, does the cabinet have inside? Are they fixed, adjustable, or a mix of the two?

☐ How many drawers, if any, does the cabinet have? Are they all the same depth, or do they vary from shallow to deep?

☐ What kind of hardware is recommended for the cabinet?

☐ Is the toeplate adjustable?

☐ Can a shallow drawer be added for height if desired?

☐ Is the surface easy to keep clean?

9 inches to 48 inches, as described above. What elevates the base cabinet to the standard height of 35 inches is the toeplate, which is usually 4½ inches high. A countertop is typically 1 to 2 inches thick; this elevates the countertop to its correct 36-37 inches in height.

You can alter the size of the toeplate, though, so that your counter can be lower or higher according to your needs. If you are very tall, you can specify the addition of a shallow drawer to elevate the cabinet still more. And, you can specify a thicker countertop to add height.

Base cabinets are commonly used to store heavy or bulky items. You can specify cabinets with pull-out shelves to reduce the strain on your back when you lean over to remove a big pot or heavy casserole. Base cabinets also may be obtained with drawers. The best of these hold drawers that range from shallow to deep; the shallowest drawer, at the top, is usually devoted to flatware.

Other base cabinets may have tilt-out

STANDARD WORK HEIGHT AND CABINET DIMENSIONS AND ADJUSTMENT OF CABINET HEIGHTS

In order to feel comfortable working at a counter, it must be the right height—for you. Standard dimensions were developed for the average person of about 5 feet 5 inches. If you are taller, raise the toeplate or add a drawer—or both—to the basic cabinet run. Remember, though, the distance between the base cabinets and wall cabinets should be 18 inches; readjust the wall cabinets so this distance stays the same.

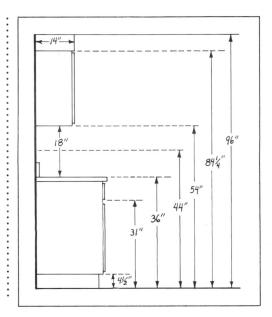

drawers; some homeowners like to keep pastry goods, such as flour, here. Other interior fittings from which to choose include dividers for separating lids or trays, bins for holding specific packaged foods, such as tall boxes of cereal or large bottles of soda, and pails for your garbage and trash.

The base cabinets that house appliances, such as a cooktop or a sink, must be selected with care; be sure you specify a cabinet that leaves just enough room all around the appliance to conform to any building code. Space for extra insulation may be required, or, conversely, an air space may be recommended for ventilation around the appliance. These base cabinets come without backs so that all hookups can be made with ease.

Corner base cabinets are a problem that can be solved in one of several ways. First, as indicated in the chapter on layouts, the

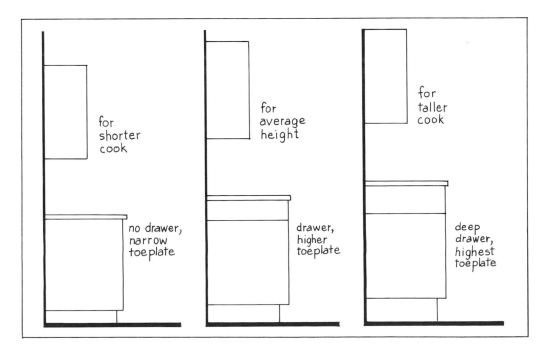

**SPECIALTY BASE CABINET
DRAWERS AND FITTINGS**

Specializing your storage
will greatly help you to
organize your supplies.
Even top-of-the-line,
ready-made cabinets can
be purchased with specialty
inserts. You must calculate
your storage needs ahead
of time, though, so that
you will know exactly what
you will want in the way of
drawers, dividers, and bins.
Esoteric fittings for spices,
cutlery, linens, and other
items can be specified.

sink may be placed in this position with the
cabinet housing it turning the corner under
the sink. Another solution is to put a base
cabinet there with a Lazy Susan. A Lazy Susan
cabinet requires at least 36 inches of wall
space in both directions. The typical Lazy
Susan has two revolving shelves. "Blind"
cabinets can be fitted into the corner, but space
here is lost back in the corner by the wall.

WALL CABINETS

Wall cabinets should match their base cabinet
counterparts in width for a balanced appearance. Wall cabinets reach 30 inches high and
are 12 inches deep. Again, like base cabinets,
they start at 9 inches in width and increase in
3-inch increments to 48 inches in width.

Wall cabinets are positioned on the wall so

LAZY SUSAN CABINET

The standard corner cabinet configuration is problematical because the corner near the wall is an unreachable ''dead'' space. A simple solution is to install a Lazy Susan cabinet. The circular shelves in this cabinet revolve, thus affording plenty of storage within the cabinet. The door on the Lazy Susan cabinet is bent at a 90-degree angle, to fit the corner turn, and it opens in either direction.

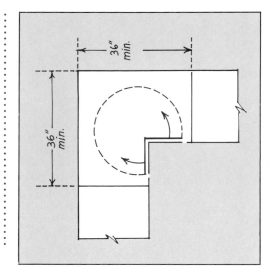

that the top of the cabinet run is 84 inches off the floor. This leaves a space of 18 inches between the bottom of the wall cabinets and the countertop. The space from the top of the cabinet to the ceiling is often filled in with a soffit, although more and more homeowners are choosing to use this area for open storage or to display decorative objects.

Special wall cabinets fit in over the refrigerator and over the range. The cabinet over the refrigerator, leaving an air space of 1 inch just above the appliance, is 15 inches high. The cabinet over the range is typically 18 inches high; this leaves enough room for an under-cabinet light and a ventilating hood to be installed.

Double access cabinets can be hung from the ceiling over a peninsula or an island. These should be hung so that there are at least 25 inches of air space over the counter. A setback of 3 inches leaves room for your head if you work at the countertop in this area.

The interiors of the wall cabinets can be outfitted for your special needs. The most basic configuration is a series of shelves.

These should be adjustable so that you can arrange foods or dishes inside to your liking. Special shelves that are narrower than the norm can be fitted onto the doors, for spices and small boxes. Can storage is another option.

If you plan to extend wall cabinets from either side of the window, be sure to leave enough space around the window for a window treatment, if you want one. Shutters, for instance, need room to fold back; curtains need space to be drawn to the sides and tied.

SPECIALTY CABINETS

Besides the specially outfitted base and wall cabinets outlined above, you can find cabinets that are tailored for very specific needs. Most of these cabinets stand 84 inches high and supplement your cabinet arrangement in the kitchen.

The most commonly requested specialty cabinet is a broom closet. A cabinet equipped with interior fittings to hold a broom, a vacuum cleaner hose, and other clean-up necessities will do the trick. Another tall cabinet that proves handy is one that holds a fold-out ironing

INSIDE NEWS

Some cabinet manufacturers offer interior configurations — working with vinylized wire baskets, bins, and shelves — that you can choose yourself. The kitchen dealer will show you the cabinet and all the interior storage options and then you can plan out the interior of the cabinet to your own specific needs. Most bins and baskets pull out for easy access; shelves are adjustable but should stay in place once installed.

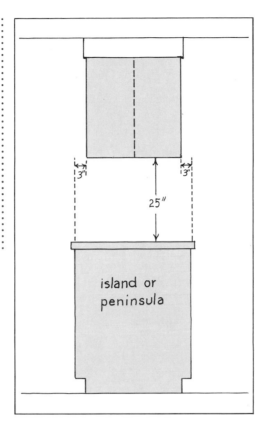

island or peninsula

board. If your kitchen has a laundry room nearby, you should consider adding this cabinet to your general order and place it near your washer and dryer.

If you have room for a pantry, tall cabinets with fold-out compartments for can storage on the doors and deeper shelves behind will organize your food. These cabinets sport double doors, so that once you open the doors, you actually have the equivalent of four separate storage zones inside.

European cabinet manufacturers make use of the soffit and the toeplate areas for additional, unexpected storage. The soffits fold down to reveal a hidden storage area

over the cabinet run. The toeplates pull out like drawers and are used for shallow storage of linens and other items that might not be used on a daily basis.

American manufacturers are taking another cue from their European counterparts: You can now find special base cabinets being designed here that enclose a hidden table. This table pulls out on casters and locks into place to be used as an extra work surface or for dining.

European manufacturers often place base cabinets — not just tables — on casters so that they can pull out from under the countertop for easy access. This is especially handy if you want to roll the trash compactor, for example, over to another area of the room.

OPEN STORAGE

Open or closed storage — or both — what do you prefer? Open storage works best as an alternative to wall cabinets. Here many people display their tablewares, enjoying the sight of their dishes and glasses as they stand in ranks along the shelves. Open storage, however, forces the homeowner to be neat and tidy and very organized.

Open storage beneath the countertop is less often in evidence in the U.S., although many European cabinetry manufacturers are showing open shelving as a link between closed base cabinets or between appliances. Again, a clean and organized look is key; disorder cannot be camouflaged!

The most common solution to open storage is to place wooden shelves on brackets, or cantilevered shelves, along the walls. Because these shelves have to be rigidly attached to the wall, they cannot be adjusted up and down once they are installed, and so you must decide ahead of time what the distance should be between shelves. To pretty up the edges of open shelves, you can attach lacy fabric or

TALL CABINETS

Tall cabinets provide the most storage in the least amount of space, especially if they are outfitted with extra pivoting shelves for cans or boxes. These shelves fold back into each other when the cabinet doors are closed. Other tall cabinets can be used for brooms and cleaning supplies or even for linens. Tall cabinets are available in standard 3-inch-wide increments from 12 inches all the way to 48 inches.

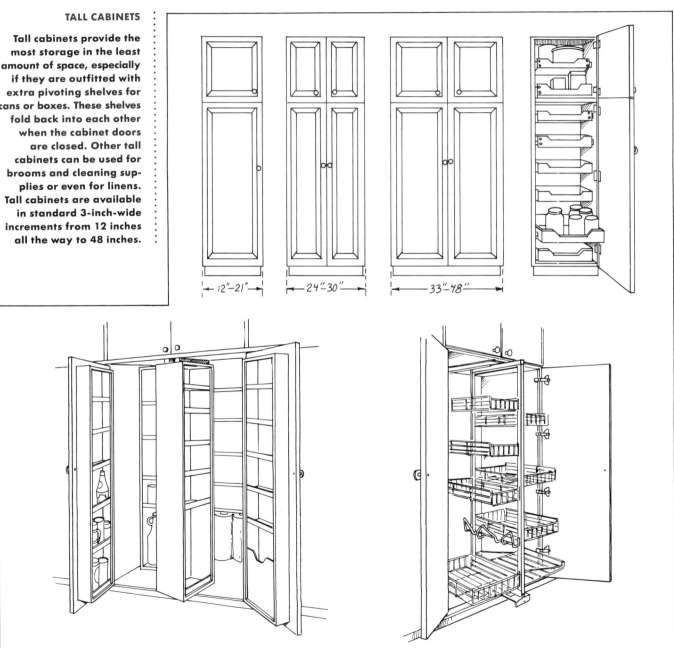

OPEN STORAGE

Open storage is personal, since you are exposing to view what you keep on hand in your kitchen. Many people love to display pots and pans and others enjoy showing off their dishes and glassware. Open shelving and pot racks are the obvious solutions to open storage, but dish drying racks are another option. For utensils, a jug or crock is a handy catch-all.

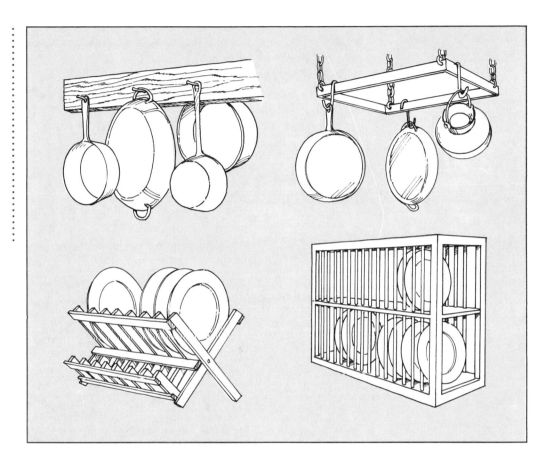

paper edging that can be easily replaced if it tears.

Two "high-tech" alternatives to wooden shelves are metal shelves or plastic-coated wire shelves. Metal shelves are available in restaurant supply shops; wire shelves are available anywhere closet supplies are sold. Plastic-coated wire grids in various sizes can be attached to the wall. These grids can be rigged with hooks, shelves, and bins to organize whatever you want to store there.

Many homeowners like to hang a butcher's rack or a pot rack from the ceiling as a catch-all for pots and pans and even for certain foods

such as sausages or garlic. Be sure the rack hangs steadily from beams in the ceiling as pots and pans can be extremely heavy. Long, single-strip pot racks can be bolted into the wall over the range or over a counter where there is no overhead storage. All pot racks come with long hooks on which to hang the various pots.

If you like to keep wooden spoons and other implements out on the counter, you can store them in jugs or crocks or other open-topped containers. Knives may come with their own hanging rack with a magnetized metal strip to keep the knives securely in place.

6 KITCHEN SURFACES AND LIGHTING

The look or style of your kitchen depends upon its surfaces and its lighting. Here you will exercise your decorative freedom to give your kitchen the mood and tone you want, be it rustic country or sleek contemporary or something in between. Keep in mind, however, that these surfaces should be easy to maintain and easy to clean. You don't want to be frustrated and hassled by such concerns as stains, grease build-up, or moisture. All of these are ongoing problems in the kitchen, but with some planning and forethought you can choose surfaces that will withstand abuse. The lighting you choose, too, will serve to enhance the decor, and so you should choose fixtures that are handsome to look at but that offer comfort for your eyes as you work and as you move throughout the room.

WALLS

Of all the surfaces in the kitchen — walls, floor, countertops, and ceiling — the walls serve as the prime decorative focus. The walls not only act as a backdrop for cabinetry and appliances but they display art and decorative items as well. Walls can be light or dark; light walls amplify light and space.

Paint

Paint is the first choice of most homeowners because it is inexpensive, easy to apply, and easy to clean. Enamel paints withstand moisture and grease far more effectively than latex; they set up a virtually indestructible seal on the wall. Latex paints, rubbery in consistency, are more porous and thus soil faster. The main problem with enamel paint is that it discolors or yellows over time in a hot environment.

Enamel paint can be cleaned with standard solvents or with cleansers. Semigloss or eggshell finishes are easier on the eyes than bright high-gloss lacquers.

The correct preparation of the walls is essential to maintenance. Be sure to seal the wall, be it plasterboard or wood, with a good primer coat. The sealant will protect against rot or mildew, especially around the range and sink.

The choice of color is, of course, up to you. You can change the "texture" of the wall, too, by using the brush or roller in inventive ways, such as stippling, sponging, or daubing. This works well when you want a more rustic look.

To calculate how much paint you need, measure the perimeter of your kitchen and multiply that figure by the height of the room. Paint typically covers about 60 square yards per gallon, but coverage will depend upon how porous or smooth the wall is. Latex paint usually covers more area than enamel paint. To be sure you have enough paint, order more than you expect you will need, especially if you will be adding a second or third coat. Colors can never be exactly or precisely matched from one batch to another, either, and so it is best to have plenty of the color you like on hand. Even if you end up with more paint than you need, the extra will come in handy for patch-ups later on.

Wallcoverings

Wallcoverings come in many styles, from miniprints to big, bold patterns. Besides style, however, it is important to choose a wallcovering that can be easily maintained. Paper wallcoverings that have not been treated against moisture will soon discolor and become stained. Vinyl-coated papers, though, can be cleaned with a damp cloth and even with a mild cleaning agent.

If you apply paper near or around a range or cooktop, apply an extra coat of moisture-resistant spray, or install a plexiglass shield as a backsplash over the paper. Grease is difficult to remove from any paper, even vinyl. Wallcoverings, though sold by the roll, are often packaged in double or even triple rolls. American wallcoverings average between 30 and 36 square feet per roll, depending upon the width of the wallcovering. Check the width of the wallcovering you like and ask about the size of the "repeat" or pattern of the design. You will have to add one or two repeats per section of wallcovering to be hung to be sure that the overall design will match up at the seams.

To calculate how much you will need, measure the perimeter of the kitchen and multiply by the height of the wall; then subtract the doors and windows and any other areas that will not be covered; divide by 30 or by 36, depending upon the amount of wall space the wallcovering will cover; add in a few inches per strip, for cutting at the top and the bottom, in case of mistakes.

Many wallcoverings are prepasted and pretrimmed, with the seams cut off, so they are very easy for do-it-yourselfers to install. The wallcoverings that are neither prepasted nor pretrimmed can be difficult to cut and fit and paste; it is recommended that these be installed by a professional paperhanger.

No wallcovering will adhere to a dirty or greasy surface. Walls must be cleaned thoroughly, and, if pitted or scarred, must be primed smooth before application of the wallcovering. If the walls are in particularly poor condition, many paperhangers suggest having the walls canvased — literally cloaked with a layer of thin canvas — to make them smooth and ready to receive a wallcovering that will not then unravel or peel over time.

WOOD WALL SURFACES

Wood as a surface acts as a ''countrified'' backdrop to the kitchen. The visual ''texture'' of the wall is created by the type of wood-joining technique used. The options include shiplap, tongue-in-groove, board-and-batten, and board-on-board. Your primary concern, no matter which joinery you prefer, is that you have a tight fit, so that no moisture or grease seeps in behind the wood.

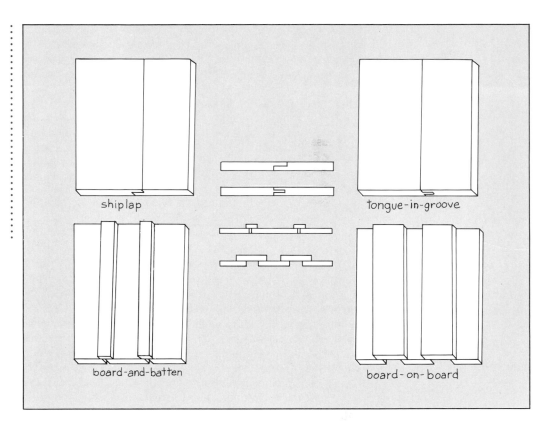

Wall Paneling

Wall paneling, durable and strong, camouflages bumpy and uneven surfaces. Wall paneling dusts easily but does not repel moisture and grease well; therefore, it is not recommended for areas around the cooking center or near the sink.

Solid wood paneling, available in planks varying in widths from 2 inches wide up to 12 inches wide, locks together either in the tongue-in-groove manner or with a shiplap edge. Woods vary in tonality from dark cedars to light pines and spruces. Planks can be installed in a number of attractive patterns: straight vertical, horizontal, diagonal stria-

tions, or herringbone. Board-and-batten and board-on-board are other variations. Because of the difficulty of creating an even surface over an uneven one, it is recommended that a professional carpenter install paneling.

Prefinished wall panels, standardized at 4 feet by 8 feet, are available in many wood looks. Most are not actually made of solid wood but of wood veneer on plywood or wood veneer on fiberboard. These may be textured and grooved to simulate planks. Textured panels attract grease build-up, so it is best to choose a smooth, vinyl-coated type. Panels are easily cut but, again, should be installed by a pro to insure an even and tight fit over the existing wall.

Ceramic Wall Tile

As an accent material, ceramic tile adds a handsome dimension to the kitchen. Whole walls of tile appear antiseptic unless they are broken up with open shelving or cabinetry or art.

Ceramic tiles work well as a backsplash because they repel moisture and wipe clean easily. If you select ceramic tile to surface the countertop, too, matching up tiles should not be difficult. Cove molding tiles and bullnose tiles finish off these surfaces for a clean look.

Wall tiles tend to be fired with a higher gloss glaze than floor tiles. They come in many colors, patterns, and textures. Hand-painted tiles are an attractive alternative — or counterpoint — to mass-produced tile.

Wall tiles are calculated in square feet; trim tile is measured by the linear foot. Tile is difficult to install because it does not budge once it is set into the adhesive. Add 10 percent to your overall quantity estimates to allow for fitting tiles into hard-to-reach areas and for breakage.

FLOORS

Because of traffic through the kitchen, the floor takes a tremendous amount of abuse. In specific activity areas where you stand, turn, and pivot, the wear increases. Chairs and stools scrape away at the floor over a period of time, too. For these reasons you should choose a thick and durable flooring surface.

In every kitchen, the flooring you select will be placed over a subfloor and, possibly, over a middle layer as well for additional support. The subfloor may be concrete or it may be plywood. Either surface is suitable, but it should be absolutely level and free of bumps.

Most flooring products can be selected at retail outlets that specialize in such products; be sure that your store offers the services of an installer, or ask them to recommend a reputable installer. Flooring, except for vinyl tile, is heavy and cumbersome to maneuver and requires professional expertise for fine results.

Your kitchen dealer, contractor, or architect, of course, can specify the flooring for you and have it installed.

Ceramic Tile

Once considered a luxury out of reach of most consumers, ceramic floor tile is becoming more affordable and plentiful in supply. Specialty and custom-designed tiles might still be the province of the elite, but mass-produced ceramic tile is now available in a full palette of hues and in a wide variety of textures and patterns. Domestic tile vies for attention with imported, both in retail outlets and in designer showrooms. Sizes and shapes vary. Most common sizes are squares measuring about 4 x 4 inches, 6 x 6 inches, 8 x 8 inches, and 12 x 12 inches. Shapes include the square, rectangle, hexagon, octagon, and the curvy-edged Spanish style called Valencia. When proportions harmonize, different sizes can be mixed together to create a dazzling effect; four 4-inch squares, for example, can intersperse with single 8-inch squares for a patchwork look. Strings of smaller tiles may border a floor of larger tiles, or vice versa.

Quarry Tile

Of all ceramics, quarry tile is probably the most popular. Quarry tiles, unglazed and in earth tones, complement any decor. Tonal variations run from pale "palomino" to deep rust or brown. Quarry tiles must be treated with a sealant, however, because they are very porous and, therefore, prone to staining and spotting by moisture and grease. Many types of quarry tile, too, are vulnerable to chipping and cracking, especially those handmade in Mexico. American quarry tiles are presealed and denser in construction, but they are less rustic in appearance because they are machine-made.

Pavers

Pavers, tiles that resemble brick, are solid and hard-wearing. They are also slip-resistant because of a rugged matte finish, and they are sealed. Pavers come in many neutral tones, including terra cotta, charcoal, gray, and gray-blue. Most are rectangular, measuring a standard 4 x 8 inches, but pavers are also available in standard-sized squares and hexagons.

Glazed Tile

Glazed tiles offer the greatest range in terms of color, texture, and pattern. When you specify glazed tile, be certain that the tile of your choice has been manufactured for installation on the floor. Many glazed tiles are produced for wall or countertop applications only. Glazed tiles can be dangerously slippery when wet; it is best to select a glaze with a rough or textured finish. You can combine tiles in several colors or mix colors with patterns. Let your imagination be your guide!

Glazed tiles come in many sizes. In the square format alone, tile runs from the 1-inch mosaic to a 12-inch square. Mosaics typically come in sheets; once the sheet is laid, grout is spread across the entire sheet, pressed into the grooves and then wiped clean.

Grouts are no longer bland gray or white; many colors are now available. Grouts can be used as a visual accent to set off tile, or they can be blended with the tile for a clear sweep of color.

Ceramic tile is complicated to install properly. Because it is heavy, ceramic tile requires a very strong foundation, a subfloor that is perfectly flat and even. Ceramic tile is difficult to cut and fit. The first tile must be centered exactly so that all the tiles visually "square off" with the room. A professional, with expertise in these matters, will do a masterful job; the task of installing tile should be left to a competent tile installer.

Brick, Slate, and Marble

Like ceramic tile, these hard surfaces require a strong subfloor. All three are porous materials and will stain easily, and marble is, in addition, extremely slippery underfoot.

Marble squares are standardized at 12 inches; slates run from 6 x 9 inches to 15 x 18 inches and can be laid in regular or random patterns. Rectangular bricks can also be laid in regular patterns; the most popular of these is the herringbone.

Cork and Linoleum

Once derided as old-fashioned, these two surfaces are coming back into vogue. Linoleums are currently imported from Europe. Cork is manufactured both here and abroad; it must be sealed because it is porous. Both cork and linoleum are easy on the feet, absorb noise, and are good surfaces for children to play on.

Sheet Vinyl

Sheet vinyls, the most comfortable flooring for the feet, cover broad expanses of floor in a single sweep. Common widths are 6, 12, and 15 feet. Sheet flooring is sold by the running foot; when you measure your floor, figure out where you want the seam — if any — to go. Also, check the pattern of your choice to gauge how much extra you will need to insure a match-up along the seam.

Vinyl flooring conforms to building codes. Thicknesses vary, though, and some sheet vinyls are cushioned for extra comfort.

The surface of the vinyl may be smooth or

HARDWOOD FLOORING

Hardwood flooring, when treated with a polyurethane sealer, is a warm-looking surface that is easy on the feet. Parquet is not recommended because there are many small pieces of wood forming the parquet squares and these may pop out with wear and tear. Narrow strips or wide planks lock together snugly and do not budge. Some versions are available for do-it-yourself installation.

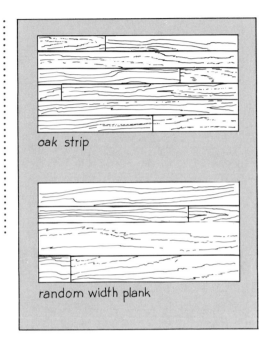

oak strip

random width plank

textured to simulate another material such as wood or slate. It may be highly glazed; highly glazed vinyls look cleaner because they are so shiny. No-wax is the norm these days; a damp mop will wipe up spills in a flash.

Most vinyl products are now guaranteed for five years against moisture damage or discoloration from mold.

Patterns are many and varied, but most do, in fact, mimic other materials such as ceramic tile.

If you are very handy, you can lay a sheet floor yourself, but cutting around obstructions is difficult, so be sure you are up to the job.

Vinyl Tile

Vinyl tiles are the easiest solution for the do-it-yourselfer. These also come in many patterns, and, once you have established the grid on your floor, are very easy to install. Be sure to select asbestos-free tiles for house-

holds with children or pets. Vinyl tiles resist moisture and stains but can scuff quite easily.

Hardwood Floors

Hardwood, as a flooring surface, is warm and resilient, comfortable underfoot, and a pleasing counterpoint to any decorating scheme.

Hardwoods, such as the perennial favorite, oak, last longer and are easier to maintain than softwoods, such as pine, which dents, splinters, and scuffs.

Oak has traditionally been sold in 2¼-inch strips, which are laid with one strip abutting the next for a smooth overall appearance. Oak strip floors, in fact, have traditionally graced many homes and, if you have inherited one, it is recommended that you simply have yours sanded and stained and sealed for your kitchen. Why replace a good thing?

New oak usually comes prepackaged in "bundles" in either a plank format or in a parquet tile. Parquet is not a good choice for the kitchen because individual pieces may pop out with wear. Planks run in three widths, and, if combined, will be termed "random-width." These widths are: 3-inch, 5-inch, and 7-inch. Some versions have straight edges and some have beveled edges which clearly define the random-width pattern as it stretches over the floor. For a rustic look, simulated dowels, or plugs, are set into the ends of the planks; these imitate the dowels that were used instead of nails in the old days.

Prepackaged hardwood flooring comes already sealed against moisture, grease, and soil build-up; you simply maintain your floor with a vacuum and a damp mop. Traditional oak strip flooring should be treated to repel moisture and grease, preferably with polyurethane.

The newest hardwood flooring products are actually laminated. A thin hardwood veneer is bonded to a double core of plywood so that it will not shrink or warp. You can find the veneered flooring surfaces in both the plank and the parquet format.

Softwoods, such as pine, which were used extensively in colonial times, are not recommended today because they dent easily. If you choose a pine floor, be sure to seal it well, as pine is far more porous than oak, and it stains readily.

COUNTERTOPS

Almost any specific kitchen task you can think of takes place on or involves a countertop: unloading groceries, preparing food and drinks, setting out and clearing dishes — even eating, if the dining setup is at a counter. Your countertops, therefore, should not only look good and fit in with your personal design scheme but they should be able to stand up to spills, cuts, chips, and other possible abuses.

If you prepare foods in a number of different ways, though, you may want to vary your countertops. You may want, for example, a chopping block area for cutting up vegetables and a marble-topped area for rolling out pastry. You will have to plan your countertop needs to match your activities — or, instead, go with a single, continuous surface and simply place other blocks or slabs on top to take care of the specialized tasks.

Consider, too, whether you want the countertop to coordinate visually with the cabinetry or if you want to set up a visual contrast.

Plastic Laminate

Less expensive than any other countertop material, plastic laminate, under a variety of brand names, comes in hundreds of colors and prints. Sophisticated photo techniques have enabled manufacturers to simulate popular natural materials such as wood, butcher block, marble, granite, and slate. Many textural effects are available as well.

Plastic laminate comes in either a glossy or a matte finish; the reflective quality of the glossy type sets up a disturbing surface glare that may hurt your eyes; still, the glossy surface is easier to wipe clean.

New solid-color laminates, with color that impregnates the entire thickness of the laminate, look good at the seams; standard laminates display a black line at the seams.

Some manufacturers offer countertops with a backsplash and bullnose trim at the front that are integral to the counter.

Plastic laminates clean easily, but they can scorch if a hot pot is placed directly on the surface. This type of countertop becomes brittle as it ages, and it can chip, dent, or crack. If you are going to do a great deal of chopping and slicing, consider adding a chopping block inlay. Some designers set the plastic laminate behind a wooden trim, too, to protect against chipping at the edge of the countertop.

Ceramic Tile

Ceramic tile for countertops has accelerated in popularity because it resists heat, is extremely durable, is compatible with ceramic tile floors, and is a versatile design element in its own right.

Smooth-surfaced machine-made tiles are easier to maintain than uneven handmade tiles. Handmade tiles tend to be more porous and vulnerable to cracking, chipping, and crackling. Because grout, the substance used to fill the space, is porous, too, it is recommended that countertop tiles be installed as closely together as possible; grout is difficult to clean. It can be sealed, though, so don't rule out grout if you love it.

Glasses and china can break on ceramic tile, too, and you should think about this hazard if you are planning to install tile countertops in a kitchen where small children will be playing.

Ceramic tiles are available in many sizes; they come from many countries, too, such as Italy, Brazil, Mexico, and Portugal. Thousands of designs are available as is a full palette of colors.

Wood

Another countertop standby, wood — especially butcher block made of maple or oak — is understandably appealing because it is a practical work surface. Concern over bacteria, which may be harbored in cracks, nicks, and crevices, has caused some states to institute laws regarding proper maintenance of wood In commercial properties. The law states that the wood must be thoroughly cleaned and sterilized often. In private residences, designers recommend that butcher block be periodically sanded and oiled to renew the surface.

Butcher block can be purchased in various widths and thicknesses and is usually ordered by the foot. Ready-made slabs are also available.

Stone

Pricey granite and marble withstand heat and chipping; marble, however, is rather porous and can stain easily, and it is difficult to clean.

Marbles come in a variety of shades, from classic white to deep green. It is best to personally choose marble to be sure you like the veining and other patterns in the stone.

Granite, which is extremely hard, stands up to abuse better than marble and is, accordingly, more expensive. Tonalities vary, but the overall look is more consistent than marble.

If you bake a great deal but cannot afford an entire countertop sheathed in stone, consider a marble or granite slab to use as an inlay.

Stainless Steel

Many professionals believe that stainless steel is the best countertop surface because it stands up to heat, staining, and cuts. Scratching the surface only enhances its patina.

Stainless steel comes in sheets which are cut to fit; trim bands of like material are fitted around the edges, or the metal can be bent around to form a self-rim around the countertop core material.

Solid Synthetic

There are so many solid synthetics entering the marketplace that it is hard to keep up with the newest patterns and textures. Once only white or marblelike, solid synthetics now simulate many textures, even stones such as granite.

Solid synthetics are not porous at all, so they repel moisture; they can also endure high temperatures and abrasion. If you do mar the surface, it can be sanded smooth again easily.

Solid synthetics may be specified with molded rims and other intricate detailing, such as inlays and special patterned effects.

Some solid synthetic countertops can be ordered with integral sinks, either in the single-bowl or the double-bowl version. And solid synthetic can be used for a complementary surface, such as a backsplash.

CEILINGS

The ceiling is usually a "given" in any room in the house. Many homeowners change the ceiling in the kitchen to enhance a particular look or style, be it contemporary or country. For a contemporary aspect, the ceiling can be dropped with recessed lighting set in at intervals to cast pools of light over specified areas in the room. For a more rustic look, by contrast, the ceiling can be opened up to expose beams and even the wood planking itself, if this exists.

Either way, the easiest solution to covering and protecting the ceiling is to cloak it with paint. A white or light-toned paint disperses light evenly throughout the kitchen and makes the room seem brighter. A smooth paint, in either a high-gloss or semigloss finish, is easiest to maintain; washing the ceiling is a chore to be avoided! Any other solution, therefore, such as a textured paint or a wall-covering, is not recommended, for these attract grease build-up over time and are difficult to sponge clean. Even exposed wood, though lovely, will be difficult to keep free of grease over the long run. Sealing the wood will help.

LIGHTING

Often ignored as a design feature in the kitchen, proper lighting is critical to comfort and efficiency. Inadequate or badly placed fixtures will cast shadows or pools of intense glare that affect the health of your eyes. Many accidents occur in the kitchen when hot foods or hot appliances are obscured by shadow. Good general illumination from the ceiling and concentrated task lighting over specific work surfaces combine to provide the best working conditions.

Lighting options are varied, but the lighting sources are just two: fluorescent and incandescent. Many homeowners opt for fluorescents because they are extremely energy-efficient. In fact, fluorescent bulbs outlive incandescents by up to five times as long. Traditionally, though, fluorescents are known to cast an unearthly glow over food so that it appears unappetizing.

Be sure to specify warm-white fluorescents so that you will obtain a light that most closely approximates natural light.

Natural light, in fact, is a prime source of illumination in the kitchen. Big windows, sky-lights, and greenhouses all serve to enhance the general atmosphere in this room.

General Lighting

General lighting diffuses best when it is directed from a ceiling fixture or from several fixtures. If the room is small, center the fixture; if the space is large, keep in mind while spacing the fixtures that an even balance of light is required throughout.

General illumination can be realized with a variety of fixtures. Pendant lights, globe lights, chandeliers, and track lighting are standard choices.

Track fittings, installed on an open channel, are versatile because the individual canisters can be moved and twisted in any direction. The open channel, however, is a prime collector of dirt and grease. Closed channel tracks are available, but the positioning of the canisters is then rigid; canisters on these tracks can be twisted but not moved.

Overhead fixtures should be outfitted with shields or shades to minimize glare. Frosted bulbs work well, too. To maximize diffusion of light throughout the kitchen, paint the ceiling in a white or off-white tone. Light-colored walls will also reflect light well. If you prefer deep-toned walls and cabinetry, you will have to amplify the light to compensate for absorption into the dark surfaces.

Some designers prefer to place overhead fixtures, especially tracks, around the perimeter of the room. If you choose to follow their example, be sure to position the track 24 inches out from the edge of the wall cabinets to offset any shadows. (When someone is standing at a work surface, a shadow will be cast by that

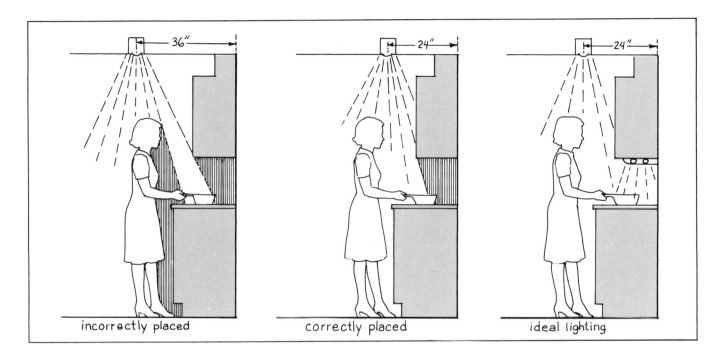

incorrectly placed   correctly placed   ideal lighting

LIGHTING COUNTERTOPS

When you stand at a counter, your body will cast a shadow on the countertop if the light fixture overhead is not correctly positioned. The correct distance for placement is 2 feet from the wall. Supplement any overhead lighting with under cabinet fixtures to be assured of adequate illumination.

person if the overhead fixture is incorrectly positioned.)

A well-lit kitchen requires at least three 150-watt incandescents or four 40-watt fluorescents to establish a comfortable lighting level.

Task Lighting

Task lighting, at each specific activity center, is crucial to efficient performance of any task, be it cooking or washing up or whatever. You need 100 watts of incandescent or 60 watts of fluorescent light for each task.

Under-cabinet lighting will effectively flood countertops if the lighting is installed as close to the front edge of the wall cabinet as possible. Long tubes work best; these should measure at least two-thirds of the length of the wall cabinet.

The light over the range may be integral to the range hood; 150 watts of incandescent or 60 watts of fluorescent light will adequately illuminate the cooking surface. If the hood does not have a light built into it, direct a spot or recessed light to the cooking surface.

At the sink, another 150 watts of incandescent or 60 watts of fluorescent will suffice. Again, a spot or recessed light will work, or another type of fixture might be selected that will add a special design accent. A window by the sink provides plenty of light on a sunny day.

Accent Lighting

Accent lighting is more decorative than functional and serves to enhance the ambience of the room. A chandelier over the dining table, for example, is a beautiful accent. Be sure you can establish an adequate lighting level for dining comfort; a dimmer or rheostat will raise or lower the light level as needed.

7 WORKING WITH PROFESSIONALS

Now that you've worked out a kitchen plan that fulfills all of your needs and dreams, it's time to grapple with the realities of getting the actual work done.

You now must analyze the scope of your project to determine who you will need to hire for the job and ultimately how much it is all going to cost. (More on that in the next chapter.)

DO I NEED TO HIRE AN ARCHITECT?

Look at the rough floor plan you have worked out for your kitchen and ask yourself these questions:

- Will I need to add on to create extra space?
- Do I want to remove walls to create extra space or open the kitchen up onto other family living areas?
- Do I want to add new walls to create new and separate areas such as a laundry room?
- Do I want to create new window or door openings?

- Do I want to install roof windows or sky-lights?

If you plan to make such structural changes in your kitchen, you'll need to hire an architect.

An architect's basic job is to prepare floor plans and specifications for the construction of your project. The architect can also be hired to supervise the entire job, from planning through construction. How much work you want the architect to do will depend on the complexity of your project and your budget.

An architect will confer with you to discuss what your needs and wants are. This is where the rough plan you've developed on the grid in the back of this book comes in. Discussing your ideas with the help of this plan will give your architect a very concrete notion of what you would like to achieve.

The architect will then prepare the actual floor plans and working drawings that will be used to build your new kitchen. First you will be presented with several ideas in sketch form. Once you have agreed on what you want, plans will be prepared in l/2-inch or

I/4-inch scale. These will include exact floor plans, elevations showing how each wall will look, and working drawings or details of any structural work that has to be done.

If you have hired your architect to supervise the entire project, he or she will help you find a qualified contractor and assist with the bidding procedure. Once the work has started, the architect will make periodic visits to the job to review the progress.

When hiring an architect, you will sign a contract that sets forth the services to be performed and the fees to be paid. If you have hired your architect to work on your project from start to finish, you can expect to pay somewhere between 8 and I5 percent of the total construction costs. This can go as high as 20 percent, however, if you've chosen a very busy or well-known architect. If you decide to hire an architect only to prepare floor plans and working drawings, and then hire and supervise the contractor on your own, a flat fee can be determined. This will be calculated on an hourly basis. You can expect to pay $50 to $75 an hour for an architect's time. A typical fee might range from $500 to $1,500.

When choosing an architect, look for a person who has done similar projects in your area. The architect who did a wonderful job in your dentist's office may not do as well with kitchen remodelings. Try to look at some of the architect's completed projects to see if his style is to your taste and to find out if previous clients have been satisfied. Also, make sure the architect is willing and able to work within your budget. It's *your* kitchen in *your* home, and so you should have the last word on how much you spend as well as on the design.

When choosing an architect, look for the letters A.I.A. after the name. This indicates membership in and accreditation by the American Institute of Architects, the professional association of architects in the U.S.

SHOULD I HIRE A KITCHEN DESIGNER INSTEAD?

Perhaps the kitchen project you are planning is somewhat modest in scale. Working with a qualified kitchen designer is the answer if:

1. You are planning no structural changes in the space but rather plan to rearrange your kitchen within the existing space.
2. You are planning to install new cabinetry, countertops, and appliances.
3. Your kitchen will be installed in a newly constructed house.

Kitchen designers often work in conjunction with cabinet dealerships. If you work with the designer at a dealership or kitchen planning center, you can also purchase the cabinets there. The design fee will be included in the price of the entire cabinetry package. Or, if you plan to buy the cabinets from another source, you can negotiate a flat fee for just the design work. The designer will charge you from $25 to $50 an hour. Average fees range from $250 to $1,000.

In either case, the designer will provide you with exact floor plans and elevations that you can give to the contractor who will do the actual work.

A kitchen cabinet dealer can provide you with stock, ready-made cabinets, or special-order, factory-built cabinets. In both cases, a wide variety of door styles and interior configurations is available. Stock cabinets will be delivered to your house ready for your contractor to install. Special-order, factory-built cabinets will usually be installed by the dealer. If you have something more unique in mind, you can hire a carpenter or cabinetmaker to build your cabinets exactly to your liking.

Also, keep in mind that it is possible to give your kitchen a face-lift without replacing all of the existing cabinets. You can change just the doors, and even if they have to be custom-made, this cost will be a fraction of the cost of replacing all of the cabinetry. Or you might consider removing only the upper cabinets and replacing them with open shelves.

When choosing a kitchen designer, look for the initials C.K.D. after his or her name. These letters indicate that this is a certified kitchen designer who has been tested and certified by the National Kitchen and Bath Association (NKBA) regarding all aspects of design and construction. A designer is qualified to take the test only after working in the industry for seven years or successfully completing a correspondence course.

Also look for the NKBA logo in the window or *Yellow Pages* ad of the kitchen dealer you choose. This indicates that the dealer is a member in good standing of the National Kitchen and Bath Association, which vouches for their reputation.

DO I NEED A GENERAL CONTRACTOR?

A general contractor is the person who will be responsible for all of the construction phases of your job from start to finish. The contractor will:

- supply the labor and materials
- schedule and coordinate the work of the various trades
- contract with and pay the various subcontractors
- obtain any building permits that are necessary if you plan to make structural changes or add living space

The contractor may hire subcontractors to do all or parts of the job, or hire workers directly.

The sequence of construction for a major kitchen remodeling is as follows:

1. Removal of old appliances, cabinets, and counters.

2. Removal of old flooring, wallcoverings, and, if necessary, ceiling and wallboard.
3. Construction of any structural changes or additions: moving walls, altering or adding window and door openings.
4. Installing new windows and doors.
5. Installing or moving wiring and plumbing.
6. Installing any built-in lighting.
7. Replacing wallboard and ceiling.
8. Installing cabinets and counters.
9. Installing plumbing fixtures and built-in appliances.
10. Installing flooring and wallcoverings.
11. Installing free-standing appliances.

If you are working in a new space, steps 1-3 can be eliminated.

Often the various subcontractors will have to return at different stages of the work. For instance, your electrician will be needed for steps 5, 6, 9, and 11. Efficient scheduling is one of the most important phases of a contractor's job.

A good general contractor with organizational experience and construction expertise can save you time and many sleepless nights. But, as with anything else, you will have to pay for this service.

The other alternative is to act as your own contractor and subcontract the job yourself. But first ask yourself, "How much time am I willing to devote to this project?" Be honest. If you're going to tackle a major remodeling and there's no one home during working hours, you'll definitely need a general contractor. If, however, someone has time to oversee and schedule the work, you might consider subcontracting the work yourself to save money. But remember, being your own general contractor is a full-time job, especially for someone who's never done it before.

Be certain that the contractor you choose is an established member of the business community in your area. Does the contractor have an office or merely an answering ser-

---

WHAT TO LOOK FOR IN A CONTRACTOR'S CONTRACT

1. Name and address of owner.
2. Name and address of contractor.
3. Address of property where work is to be done.
4. Time work is scheduled to begin.
5. Time work is scheduled to be completed.
6. List of drawings and materials to be used to complete the job.
7. Price of the work.
8. Schedule of payment.
9. Terms of guarantee for the work.
10. Proof of workmen's compensation insurance.
11. Signature of both parties.
12. No blank spaces should be left which could be filled in later.

There should be two signed copies of the contract, one for the owner and one for the contractor. Standard contracts can be ordered from: Wilhelm Publishing, PO Box 922, Columbia, Missouri 65205.

---

vice and mail drop? Ask to speak to past customers; were they satisfied with the contractor's performance, in terms of both quality and schedule? Also ask if you might see some finished projects.

You can also check with the Better Business Bureau or Chamber of Commerce to see if there is an adverse file or record.

As with an architect, you will sign a contract with your general contractor setting forth all responsibilities, including a list of materials the contractor is expected to supply. The contract will also include a payment schedule and the total price of the job. You can typically expect to pay 20 percent to 25 percent down and l5 percent to 20 percent once the job is satisfactorily completed. The balance can be divided into two to three payments, to be made every three to four weeks, depending on the length of the job. Make sure that all of the work is guaranteed and that the terms of the guarantee are spelled out.

For a free pamphlet on choosing a contractor, send a self-addressed, stamped envelope to: NARI (National Association of the Remodeling Industry), l901 North Moore Street, Suite 808, Arlington, Virginia 22209.

WHAT IF I WANT TO SUBCONTRACT MY OWN JOB?

The only way to do this is to hire separate subcontractors for each part of the work, with each supplying all of the labor and materials needed for each specific assignment. All of the subcontractors will have to be hired and evaluated separately, and they will all need their own contracts and their own sets of working drawings. The list of subcontractors you'll need for a job of any size can be formidable: carpenter, electrician (who'll also install your electrical appliances), plumber, countertop fabricator/installer, tile layer, floor installer, painter, and wallpaperer.

If you're handy with tools, you'll probably be tempted to do some of the work yourself. Again, be realistic about what you can expect to accomplish. Rather than trying to tackle the whole job, for instance, plan on doing some of the finishing work, like painting or laying the floors, which can be done when the rest of the job is completed. That way you can work at your own pace and not hold up the workers you've hired, which might incur extra expense.

8 PLANNING THE BUDGET

Kitchen remodelings can run from a few thousand dollars to a hundred thousand or more. Where your project will fall in this spectrum depends on the most basic question: How much do you want to spend?

ESTABLISHING A BUDGET

Some questions to consider in making this decision are:

- Do I only want to commit funds I now have available?
- Am I willing to take out a home improvement loan?
- Do I want to consider refinancing my home and making a major reinvestment to increase its resale value?

Major kitchen remodelings are one of the better home improvement investments. They can return 70 to 90 percent of the amount invested at the time of resale. But you'll also want to consider the amount you want to invest in relation to the total value of your home. It would be foolish to invest $50,000, for example, to redo a kitchen in a home that couldn't be expected to sell for more than $100,000. At the same time, the installation of new, but economy priced, appliances and cabinets in a $250,000 house wouldn't increase its value. This would, therefore, be a waste of time and money.

ALLOCATING EXPENSES

The list of possible expenditures that will make up your budget will include:

1. Architect's fee (either a flat fee or 8 to 10 percent of the total cost).
2. Kitchen designer's fee (same as above).
3. The cost of all new cabinets, appliances, countertops, sinks, flooring, and lighting fixtures, as well as any windows, doors, or skylights.
4. General contractor's fee (the contractor will add 15 to 25 percent of the cost into the estimate to cover this).
5. Labor and additional materials provided by the subcontractors (for instance, plumbers, electricians, carpenters, tile layers, floor

SAMPLE EXPENSES

	Economy	Good	Better	The Very Best
Cabinets	$4,000-$8,000	$6,000-$12,000	$10,000-$25,000	$25,000-$50,000
Countertops	$250-$750	$500-$1,000	$1,000-$2,000	$1,750-$5,000
Appliances	$1,350-$2,000	$2,000-$3,000	$3,250-$6,750	$8,000-$20,750
Totals	$5,600-$10,750	$8,500-$16,000	$14,250-$33,750	$34,750-$75,750

installers, and countertop fabricators). Keep in mind that every service you require, every extra change you make, in fact, every pipe you move or wire you have installed, will add to the total cost.

Before you start asking for bids from architects or contractors, you should determine a preliminary budget for the items listed in step 3 above. These prices are easier to nail down and tend to fluctuate much less than those for labor or design services.

With the plan you've worked out on the grid in the back of this book, do some comparison shopping. First visit several kitchen cabinet showrooms in your area. Choose some cabinet styles you like and ask the dealer to give you a *ballpark figure* for a kitchen of the size you project. Then go to the appliance and plumbing suppliers. Choose two or three models of each piece of equipment you'll need. Jot down the price and the list of features each model offers. At a building supply dealer, do the same for flooring and countertop material, as well as any windows, doors, and skylights you'd like to use. And a visit to a lighting supply house will give an idea of lighting costs.

Once you're back home, make up lists of the different possible equipment combinations and the prices — good, better, ideal. Add up the total cost. See the box entitled Sample Expenses for an idea of what these costs might be. Double each estimate to account for labor and additional materials and you will have an approximation of what the project will cost.

You are now ready to talk to an architect — if you'll need one — or directly to possible contractors. Show them your rough floor plan and your material lists. Then ask them for an estimate of the cost of the project. Remember, however, that without final floor plans, working drawings, and specifications, even these experts can at best give you a "guess-timate" of the construction costs.

Labor prices fluctuate greatly from one part of the country to another, whereas material costs tend to be more consistent from coast to coast. A carpenter in metropolitan·Boston will probably charge twice the hourly rate of someone in Birmingham, Alabama. It is, therefore, impossible to give exact average prices for remodelings that might apply across the country. If you are planning to replace your appliances as well as counters, wallcoverings, and floor, but *not* cabinets, expect to pay between $6,000 and $12,000. With the addition of new cabinets, the cost can jump between $15,000 to $30,000. If you're also planning structural changes or additions, prices can go as high as $50,000 to $75,000. And if only the top-of-the-line will do for you, you could spend $100,000 or more.

When you add your total materials cost to the "guess-timates" on construction costs, you will have a very rough idea of what you're getting into. If this amount is way over or way under what you're ready to spend, reevaluate your decisions about the scope of your project and the equipment you have chosen and adjust the expected expenditure accordingly.

GETTING BIDS

Once you come up with a rough estimate that falls within your budget, you are ready to proceed with soliciting actual bids.

As stated above, this can only be done once final building plans have been prepared by an architect or kitchen designer.

You should get bids from more than one contractor for your project in order to get the best possible price. The standard number is three; the contractor should have some assurance he or she has a chance of getting the job.

A copy of the complete set of plans you have received from your architect or developer should be sent to each bidder. You can expect to wait from two to four weeks to receive your bids. A contractor needs to assess the project properly, based on the plans, in order to draw up all anticipated costs.

The usual method of bidding on remodeling projects and new construction is fixed-price bidding, as opposed to cost-plus estimates. This means that the contractor, after studying your construction plans, has estimated the cost to do the work, added in a profit, and come up with a cost for the job to be done. Once the contract is signed, the contractor is obligated to perform the work specified in the contract for the price agreed upon. If, however, you decide on any changes after the contract is signed, the contractor is given the chance to alter the estimate.

You may receive widely varying bids on your remodeling job. The most expensive bid may not guarantee the best work. That contractor may have high overhead, use union employees, or the job may just come at a busy time, resulting in the need to hire extra workers or pay overtime. Conversely, a low bid may be submitted by someone who needs the work at the moment or does some of the work personally. Discuss the bids you receive with the potential contractors if you feel they are not in line. Find out what the reasons are.

Most importantly, allow enough time to evaluate the people you plan to hire, to work out your budget, accept bids, and carefully read all of the contracts you sign. A little extra time devoted to these details before the actual construction begins can often spare you many headaches later down the line.

Directory of Resources

This resource directory lists over 170 national manufacturers who supply all the basic building materials needed for a kitchen installation. The categories include appliances, cabinet manufacturers, plumbing fixtures, surfacing materials (for floors, countertops, and walls), windows (including patio doors and skylights), and miscellaneous accessories.

APPLIANCES

In the following listing a full line of appliances includes electric and gas cooking equipment, refrigerators, and dishwashers.

AEG
ANDI-CO. Appliances
65 Campus Plaza
Edison, New Jersey 08837
(201) 225-8837
built-in appliances including electric and gas cooktops, electric wall ovens, microwaves, refrigerators, freezers, dishwashers, laundry equipment

AGA Cookers
Cooper & Turner, Inc.
R.F.D. 1, Box 477
Stowe, Vermont 05672
(802) 253-9729
unique gas- and coal-fired cast iron stoves

Admiral Co.
1701 E. Woodfield Road
Schaumburg, Illinois 60196
(312) 884-2600
full line, plus freezers, built-in refrigerators; also produces Norge brand electric and gas cooking equipment, refrigerators, freezers; and Warwick brand refrigerators and freezers

Amana Refrigeration, Inc.
Amana, Iowa 52204
(319) 622-5511
electric cooking equipment, refrigerators, freezers, dishwashers, microwaves

Caloric Corp.
403 N. Main Street
Topton, Pennsylvania 19562-1499
(215) 682-4211
full line, plus microwaves and compactors; also produces Modern Maid brand electric and gas cooking equipment, dishwashers, microwaves, compactors

Dacor
950 S. Raymond Avenue
Pasadena, California 91105
(213) 682-2803
gas and electric cooking equipment

Elmira Stove Works
22 Church Street W.
Elmira, Ontario
CANADA N3B 1M3
(519) 669-5103
traditional wood- and coal-burning cast-iron stoves,
and electric range in old-fashioned cast-iron stove
body

Gaggenau USA Corp.
5 Commonwealth Avenue
Woburn, Massachusetts 01801
(617) 938-1655
built-in electric and gas cooktops, electric ovens

Garland Commercial Industries
185 E. South Street
Freeland, Pennsylvania 18224
(717) 636-1000
commercial gas ranges

General Electric
Louisville, Kentucky 40225
800-626-2000
full line, plus freezers, microwaves, compactors,
laundry equipment; also produces Hotpoint brand
full line, plus freezers, microwaves, compactors,
laundry equipment

The House of Webster
PO Box 488
Rogers, Arkansas 72756
(501) 636-4640
electric range and electric wall oven in old-fashioned
cast iron replicas

In-Sink-Erator
Emerson Electric Co.
4700-21st Street
Racine, Wisconsin 53406
800-558-5712
dishwashers, compactors

Jenn-Air Co.
3035 Shadeland
Indianapolis, Indiana 46226
(317) 545-2271
full line, plus freezers, microwaves, compactors

Sears
Kenmore
Sears Tower
Department 703
Chicago, Illinois 60684
(312) 875-2500
full line, plus freezers, microwaves, compactors,
laundry equipment

KitchenAid, Inc.
701 Main Street
St. Joseph, Michigan 49085
(616) 982-4500
full line, plus freezers, microwaves, compactors

Magic Chef Co.
740 King Edward Avenue
Cleveland, Tennessee 37311
(615) 472-3372
full line, plus freezers, microwaves, compactors;
also produces Gaffers & Sattler brand full line, plus
freezers and microwaves; and Hardwick brand
electric and gas ranges

Maytag Co.
One Dependability Square
Newton, Iowa 50208
(515) 792-7000
electric and gas cooking equipment, dishwashers,
microwaves, laundry equipment

Miele Appliances, Inc.
22D Worlds Fair Drive
Somerset, New Jersey 08873
(201) 560-0899
built-in appliances, including electric cooktops,
electric ovens, dishwashers, laundry equipment

Panasonic
1 Panasonic Way
Secaucus, New Jersey 07094
(201) 348-7000
electric cooking equipment, refrigerators, freezers,
dishwashers, microwaves

Quasar Co.
1325 Pratt Boulevard
Elk Grove Village, Illinois 60007
(312) 228-3640
refrigerators, microwaves

Roper Corp.
PO Drawer R
Lafayette, Georgia 30728
(404) 638-4651
full line, plus microwaves, compactors

Sanyo Electric, Inc.
200 Riser Road
Little Ferry, New Jersey 07643
(201) 641-2333
refrigerators, freezers, microwaves, laundry
equipment

Speed Queen
PO Box 990
Ripon, Wisconsin 54971
(414) 748-3121
laundry equipment

Sub-Zero Freezer Co.
PO Box 4130
Madison, Wisconsin 53711
(608) 271-2233
built-in refrigerators and freezers

Thermador
5119 District Boulevard
Los Angeles, California 90040
(213) 562-1133
built-in electric and gas cooktops, wall ovens,
dishwashers, microwaves

Toshiba America, Inc.
82 Totowa Road
Wayne, New Jersey 07470
(201) 628-8000
refrigerators, microwaves, laundry equipment

Traulsen & Co., Inc.
114-02 15th Avenue
College Point, New York 11356
(718) 463-9000
commercial and commercial-style refrigerators
and freezers

TuliKivi
Box 300
Schuyler, Virginia 22969
(804) 831-2228
soapstone wood-burning cookstoves and bake
ovens

Viking Range Corp.
PO Box 8012
Greenwood, Mississippi 38930
(601) 455-1200
commercial-style gas ranges for residential use

Vulcan-Hart Corp.
PO Box 696
Louisville, Kentucky 40201
(502) 778-2791
commercial gas ranges

WCI Appliance Group
WCI Major Appliance Center
300 Phillipi Road
Columbus, Ohio 43228
(614) 272-4235
produces the following brands of appliances:

Gibson
800-458-1445
full line, plus freezers, laundry equipment

Kelvinator
800-323-7773
electric cooking equipment, refrigerators,
freezers, dishwashers, laundry equipment

O'Keefe & Merritt
full line, plus microwaves, compactors

Philco
refrigerators, freezers, laundry equipment

Tappan
800-537-5530
full line, plus microwaves, compactors, laundry
equipment

White-Westinghouse
800-245-0600
full line, plus freezers, microwaves, laundry
equipment

Whirlpool Corp.
2000 M63 North
Benton Harbor, Michigan 49022
800-253-1301
full line, plus freezers, microwaves, laundry
equipment

Wolf Range Co.
19600 S. Alameda Street
PO Box 7050
Compton, California 90224
(213) 774-7565
commercial gas ranges

CABINETS

All the following manufacturers produce a variety of door styles, ranging from traditional wood to European-style laminate, unless otherwise indicated.

ALNO Kitchen Cabinets, Inc.
385 Bellevue Drive
Newark, Delaware 19713
(302) 366-8592
custom European cabinetry

Allmilmo Corp.
70 Clinton Road
Fairfield, New Jersey 07006
(201) 227-2502
custom European cabinetry

Aristokraft Cabinets
One Aristokraft Square
Jasper, Indiana 47546
(812) 482-2527
stock cabinetry

Robert Bosch Sales Corp.
2800 S. 25th Avenue
Broadview, Illinois 60153
(312) 865-5200
custom European cabinetry

Capri Custom Cabinetry, Inc.
59 Armstrong Road
Plymouth, Massachusetts 02360
(617) 746-4912
custom cabinetry

Excel Wood Products Co., Inc.
One Excel Plaza
Lakewood, New Jersey 08701
(201) 364-2000
stock cabinetry

Fieldstone Cabinet Co.
PO Box 109
Highway 105 E.
Northwood, Iowa 50459
(515) 324-2114
custom cabinetry

Haas Cabinet Co., Inc.
625 W. Utica Street
Sellersburg, Indiana 47172
(812) 246-4431
stock and custom wood cabinetry

HomeCrest Corp.
1002 Eisenhower Drive N.
PO Box 595
Goshen, Indiana 46526
(219) 533-9571
stock cabinetry

Kountry Kraft Kitchen, Inc.
Box 882, RD 2
Newmanstown, Pennsylvania 17073
(215) 589-4575
custom cabinetry

Kraft Maid Cabinetry, Inc.
16052 Industrial Parkway
PO Box 1055
Middlefield, Ohio 44062
(216) 632-5333
stock cabinetry

Läger Kitchens
35 Agnes Street
East Providence, Rhode Island 02914
(401) 438-8320
custom European cabinetry

Merillat Industries, Inc.
5353 W. US 223
PO Box 1946
Adrian, Michigan 49221
(517) 263-0771
stock cabinetry

Millbrook Kitchens, Inc.
Box 21, Route 20
Nassau, New York 12123
(518) 766-3033
custom cabinetry

Plato Woodwork, Inc.
PO Box 117
Plato, Minnesota 55370
(612) 238-2193
custom wood cabinetry

Poggenpohl USA Corp.
6 Pearl Court
Allendale, New Jersey 07401
(201) 934-1511
custom European cabinetry

Quaker Maid
State Route 61
Leesport, Pennsylvania 19533
(215) 926-3011
custom cabinetry

Rich Craft Custom Kitchens, Inc.
141 W. Penn Avenue
Robesonia, Pennsylvania 19551
(215) 693-5871
custom cabinetry

Rutt Custom Kitchens
Route 23
Goodville, Pennsylvania 17528
(215) 445-6751
custom cabinetry

H. J. Scheirich Co.
250 Ottawa Avenue
PO Box 37120
Louisville, Kentucky 40233
(502) 363-3583
stock cabinetry

SieMatic
One Neshaminy Interplex
Suite 207
Trevose, Pennsylvania 19047
(215) 244-0700
custom cabinetry

Smallbone Traditional English Kitchens
150 E. 58th Street
Suite 904
New York, New York 10155
(212) 935-3222
custom cabinetry made from new and old recycled
wood, and with custom painted finishes

Whirlpool Kitchens, Inc.
6300 S. Syracuse Way
Suite 700
Englewood, Colorado 80111
(303) 740-3800
custom steel-frame cabinetry

Wood-Mode Cabinetry
1 Second Street
Kreamer, Pennsylvania 17833
(717) 374-2711
custom cabinetry

Yorktowne Cabinets
PO Box 231
Red Lion, Pennsylvania 17356
(717) 244-4011
stock cabinetry

PLUMBING FIXTURES

The manufacturers listed produce sinks,
faucets, hot water dispensers, garbage disposals, and water filtration systems.

ABBAKA
435 23rd Street
San Francisco, California 94107
(415) 648-7210
stainless steel, brass, and enameled sinks, and
faucets

ALAPE
8630 E. 33rd Street
Indianapolis, Indiana 46226
(317) 897-1142
enameled sinks, faucets

American Standard, Inc.
U.S. Plumbing Products
PO Box 6820
Piscataway, New Jersey 08855
(201) 980-3000
enameled cast-iron and enameled steel sinks,
faucets

Amway Corp.
7575 E. Fulton Road
Ada, Michigan 49355
(616) 676-6000
water treatment systems

Caloric Corp.
403 N. Main Street
Topton, Pennsylvania 19562-1499
(215) 682-4211
Caloric and Modern Maid brand garbage disposals

The Chicago Faucet Co.
2100 S. Nuclear Drive
Des Plaines, Illinois 60018
(312) 694-4400
old-fashioned kitchen and bar faucets

Culligan International Co.
1 Culligan Parkway
Northbrook, Illinois 60062
(312) 498-2000
water treatment systems

Delta Faucet Co.
55 E. 111th Street
PO Box 40980
Indianapolis, Indiana 46280
(317) 848-1812
traditional and single-handled sink and bar faucets

E.I. Dupont de Nemours & Co.
Corian Building Products
1007 Market Street
Wilmington, Delaware 19898
800-441-7515
solid synthetic sinks, one-piece sink/countertop products

EPIC
8630 E. 33rd Street
Indianapolis, Indiana 46226
(317) 897-1142
faucets, soap dispensers

Elkay Manufacturing
2222 Camden Court
Oak Brook, Illinois 60521
(312) 574-8484
stainless steel sinks, faucets, instant hot water dispensers, chilled water dispensers

Franke, Inc.
Kitchen Systems Division
Box 428
Hatfield, Pennsylvania 19440
800-626-5771
stainless steel and enameled kitchen and bar sinks, faucets

Grohe America, Inc.
900 Lively Boulevard
Wood Dale, Illinois 60191
(312) 350-2600
kitchen faucets, faucets with built-in water filtration systems

Gustavsberg U.S.A., Inc.
3129 Pinewood
PO Box 300457
Holtom, Texas 76010
(817) 831-4379
Amerite compressed quartz sinks

In-Sink-Erator Division
Emerson Electric Co.
4700-21st Street
Racine, Wisconsin 53406
800-558-5712
garbage disposals, hot water dispensers

Jenn-Air Co.
3035 Shadeland
Indianapolis, Indiana 46226
(317) 545-2271
garbage disposals

KitchenAid, Inc.
701 Main Street
St. Joseph, Michigan 49085
(616) 982-4500
garbage disposals

Kohler Co.
Kohler, Wisconsin 53044
(414) 457-4441
enameled cast-iron sinks, faucets

Luwa Corp.
PO Box 16348
Charlotte, North Carolina 28297
(704) 394-8341
stainless steel, brass, and enameled sinks, faucets

Magic Chef, Inc.
740 King Edward Avenue
Cleveland, Tennessee 37311
(615) 472-3372
Magic Chef and Gaffers & Settler brand garbage disposals

Maytag Co.
One Dependability Square
Newton, Iowa 50208
(515) 792-7000
garbage disposals

NIBCO, Inc.
500 Simpson Avenue
PO Box 1167
Elkhart, Indiana 46515
(219) 295-3000
washerless faucets

Price Pfister
13500 Paxton Street
Pacoima, California 91331
(818) 896-1141
single-lever, two-handled sink faucets, bar faucets

RainSoft
2080 Lunt Avenue
Elk Grove Village, Illinois 60007
(312) 439-9151
water treatment systems

Stanadyne/Moen, Inc.
377 Woodland Avenue
Elyria, Ohio 44036
(216) 323-3341
stainless steel sinks, faucets

Villeroy & Boch
Interstate 80 at New Maple Avenue
Pine Brook, New Jersey 07058
(201) 575-0550
ceramic sinks

WCI Appliance Group
WCI Major Appliance Center
300 Phillipi Road
Columbus, Ohio 43228
(614) 272-4235
Frigidaire, O'Keefe & Merritt, Tappan, and White-Westinghouse brand garbage disposals

SURFACING MATERIALS

Listed below are the major manufacturers of flooring and countertop materials, as well as some specialty products for walls and ceilings.

AA-Abbingdon Affiliates, Inc.
2149 Utica Avenue
Brooklyn, New York 11234
(718) 258-8333
tin ceilings and cornices

Aged Woods
147 W. Philadelphia Street
York, Pennsylvania 17403
800-233-9307
old wood recycled into wide-plank flooring and panelings, full line of hand-hewn beams and rafters

American Olean Tile Co., Inc.
PO Box 271
Lansdale, Pennsylvania 19446
(215) 855-1111
ceramic mosaic tile, glazed wall and floor tile, quarry tile, marble tile

Armstrong World Industries, Inc.
PO Box 3001
Lancaster, Pennsylvania
800-233-3823
vinyl sheet flooring and vinyl tile for do-it-yourself and professional installations; ceiling systems

Avonite, Inc.
12836 Arroyo Street
Sylmar, California 91342
800-4-AVONITE
800-554-6503 in California
solid synthetic countertops

Azrock Industries, Inc.
PO Box 34030
San Antonio, Texas 78265
(512) 341-5101
sheet vinyl and vinyl tile flooring

Bangkok Industries, Inc.
Gillingham & Worth Streets
Philadelphia, Pennsylvania 19124
(215) 537-5800
exotic hardwood flooring in prefinished and unfinished plank, strip, and parquet patterns, ornamental border patterns

Bangor Cork Co., Inc.
William & D Streets
Pen Argyl, Pennsylvania 18072
(215) 863-9041
true linoleum imported from Holland

Bruce Hardwood Floors
16803 Dallas Parkway
PO Box 220100
Dallas, Texas 75222-0100
(214) 931-3000
prefinished and unfinished hardwood floors in plank and parquet patterns

Carlisle Restoration Lumber
Rt. No. 123
Stoddard, New Hampshire 03464
(603) 446-3937
wide-plank pine or oak boards

Color Tile
515 Houston Street
Fort Worth, Texas 76102
(817) 870-9400
ceramic floor and wall tiles

Congoleum Corp.
195 Belgrove Drive
Kearny, New Jersey 07021
(201) 991-1000
sheet vinyl and vinyl tile flooring

Designs in Tile
PO Box 4983, Dept. CO3
Foster City, California 94404
(415) 571-7122
historic reproduction ceramic tile

E.I. Dupont de Nemours & Co.
Corian Building Products
1007 Market Street
Wilmington, Delaware 19898
800-441-7515
solid synthetic countertops

Dutch Products & Supply Co.
166 Lincoln Avenue
Yardley, Pennsylvania 19067
(215) 493-4873
complete line of Royal Delft tiles

Elon, Inc.
150 E. 58th Street
New York, New York 10155
(212) 759-6996
handmade Mexican glazed and unglazed terra
cotta tile

Florida Tile
PO Box 447
Lakeland, Florida 33802
(813) 687-7171
glazed wall and floor tiles

Formica Corp.
One Stanford Road
PO Box 338
Piscataway, New Jersey 08854
(201) 469-1555
decorative laminates

Georgia-Pacific
133 Peachtree Street N.E.
Atlanta, Georgia 30303
800-447-2882
800-322-4400 in Illinois
paneling, wood moldings

Hoboken Wood Floors Corp.
100 Willow Street
PO Box 510
East Rutherford, New Jersey 07073
(201) 933-9700
hardwood flooring in plank, parquet, and strip
patterns

Kentucky Wood Floors
PO Box 33276
Louisville, Kentucky 40232
(502) 451-6024
unfinished plank, parquet, and strip patterns,
custom designs

Mannington Mills, Inc.
PO Box 30
Salem, New Jersey 08079
(609) 935-3000
sheet vinyl and vinyl tile flooring

Marble Technics, Ltd.
150 E. 58th Street
New York, New York 10155
(212) 750-9189
marble, limestone, and granite tiles

Masonite Corp.
1 S. Wacker Drive
Chicago, Illinois 60606
(312) 750-0900
hardboard paneling

Memphis Hardwood Flooring Co.
PO Box 7253
Memphis, Tennessee 38107
(901) 526-7306
hardwood flooring

Mid-State Tile
PO Box 1777
Lexington, North Carolina 27292
(704) 249-3931
glazed wall and floor tile, quarry tile

Mountain Lumber Co., Inc.
Rt. 2, Box 43-1
Ruckersville, Virginia 22968
(804) 985-3646
heart pine flooring and paneling, hand-hewn
ceiling beams

Nevamar Corp.
8339 Telegraph Road
Odenton, Maryland 21113
(301) 569-5000
solid synthetic countertop materials, decorative
laminates

W. F. Norman Corp.
PO Box 323
Nevada, Missouri 64772
800-641-4038
metal ceilings, wainscoting, wall panels, cornices, moldings

Old Carolina Brick Co.
Rt. 9, Box 77 Majolica Road
Salisbury, North Carolina 28144
(704) 636-8850
hand-molded bricks, pavers

Pittsburgh Corning Corp.
800 Presque Isle Drive
Pittsburgh, Pennsylvania 15239
(412) 327-6100
glass bricks

Robbins, Inc.
4777 Eastern Avenue
Cincinnati, Ohio 45226
(513) 871-8988
prefinished hardwood floors in plank and parquet patterns

Southington Specialty Wood Co.
835 W. Queen Street
Southington, Connecticut 06489
(203) 621-6787
flooring milled to order in oak, ash, cherry, maple

States Industries, Inc.
PO Box 7037
Eugene, Oregon 97401
800-547-8928
beaded paneling for wainscoting and ceilings, finished and unfinished

Summitville Tiles, Inc.
Summitville, Ohio 43962
(216) 223-1511
ceramic mosaic tile, glazed wall and floor tile, quarry tile

Tarkett, Inc.
PO Box 264
800 Lanidex Plaza
Parsippany, New Jersey 07054
(201) 428-9000
sheet vinyl and vinyl tile flooring, prefinished and unfinished hardwood flooring in plank and parquet patterns

Terra Designs
241 E. Blackwell Street
Dover, New Jersey 07801
(201) 539-2999
hand-decorated wall and floor tiles, custom designs

V-T Industries, Inc.
1000 Industrial Park
Holstein, Iowa 51025
800-882-7732
(712) 368-4381 in Iowa
ready-made countertops

Vermont Soapstone Co.
RR 1, Box 514
Perkinsville, Vermont 05151
(802) 263-5404
custom-cut soapstone for sinks, countertops

Vermont Structural Slate Co., Inc.
PO Box 98
Fair Haven, Vermont 05743
800-343-1900
slate flooring, countertops

Villeroy & Boch
Interstate 80 at New Maple Avenue
Pine Brook, New Jersey 07058
(201) 575-0550
glazed and unglazed wall and floor tile

Ralph Wilson Plastics Co.
600 General Bruce Drive
Temple, Texas 76501
800-433-3222
800-792-6000 in Texas
Wilsonart brand decorative laminates

Walker Zanger
1832 S. Brand Boulevard
Glendale, California 91204
(213) 245-6927
imported glazed and unglazed wall and floor tile

WINDOWS, PATIO DOORS, GREENHOUSES

This category includes the major manufacturers of windows for new and retrofitted installations. Patio door and skylight suppliers are also listed.

Andersen Corp.
Bayport, Minnesota 55003
(612) 439-5150
vinyl-clad windows, sliding patio doors

Atrium Door & Window Corp.
PO Box 226957
Dallas, Texas 75222
(214) 634-9663
wood swinging patio doors, windows

Caradco Corp.
PO Box 920
Rantoul, Illinois 61866
(217) 893-4444
windows with baked-on coating on exterior frames

Creative Structures, Inc.
1765 Walnut Lane
Quakertown, Pennsylvania 18951
(215) 538-2426
redwood-framed Solarwall, skylights, solar room additions

Crestline
910 Cleveland Avenue
Wausau, Wisconsin 54401
(715) 845-1161
wood windows with authentic divided lights

Four Seasons Solar Products Corp.
5005 Veterans Memorial Highway
Holbrook, New York 11741
(516) 563-4000
solar room additions

Hurd Millwork Co.
520 S. Whelen Avenue
Medford, Wisconsin 54451
(715) 748-2011
aluminum-clad windows, sliding patio doors

Living Windows
PO Box 36447
Houston, Texas 77236
(713) 497-8300
aluminum-frame windows and patio doors, greenhouse windows

Lord & Burnham
Box 255
Irvington, New York 10533
(914) 591-8800
greenhouses, greenhouse windows

Marvin Windows
PO Box 100
Warroad, Minnesota 56763
800-346-5128
800-552-1167 in Minnesota
stock and made-to-order wood windows for retrofitting and new construction

Morgan Products, Ltd.
PO Box 2446
601 Oregon Street
Oshkosh, Wisconsin 54903
(414) 435-7464
wood-frame swinging and sliding patio doors, french doors

Peachtree Windows and Doors
Box 5700
Norcross, Georgia 30091
(404) 497-2000
tubular aluminum exterior framed windows and sliding patio doors with wood interior frames

Pella Windows and Doors
100 Main Street
Pella, Iowa 50219
(515) 628-1000
aluminum exterior frame windows and sliding patio doors

Pozzi Window Co.
PO Box 5249
62845 Boyd Acres Road
Bend, Oregon 97708
800-547-6880
(503) 389-7971 in Oregon
wood-frame and aluminum-clad windows, sliding and swinging patio doors

Roto Frank of America, Inc.
PO Box 599
Research Park
Chester, Connecticut 06412
(203) 526-4996
roof windows

Velux-America, Inc.
PO Box 3208
Greenwood, South Carolina 29648
(803) 223-3149
skylights, roof windows

Weathervane
10819 120th Avenue N.E.
Kirkland, Washington 98033
(206) 827-9669
super air-tight wood windows

Webb Manufacturing
PO Box 707
Conneaut, Ohio 44030
(216) 593-1151
round, oval, half-round, and quarter-round windows

MISCELLANEOUS ACCESSORIES

This section includes sources for decorative
hardware, lighting fixtures, venting systems,
ceiling fans and storage devices, as well as
sources for reproduction moldings and nails.

ABBAKA
435 23rd Street
San Francisco, California 94107
(415) 648-7210
brass hoods

Baldwin Hardware
841 Wyomissing Boulevard
Reading, Pennsylvania 19603
(215) 777-7811
solid brass hardware

Ball & Ball
463 W. Lincoln Highway
Exton, Pennsylvania 19341
(215) 363-7330
reproduction Early American hardware

Broan Manufacturing Co., Inc.
Hartford, Wisconsin 53027
(414) 673-4340
range hoods, kitchen fans

Casablanca Fan Co.
PO Box 424
City of Industry, California 91747
(818) 369-6441
ceiling fans

Clairson International
720 S.W. 17th Street
Ocala, Florida 32674
(904) 351-6100
Closet Maid brand vinyl-coated wire storage
organizers

Comalco International
PO Box 675
Perrysburg, Ohio 43551
(419) 666-8700
Calphalon brand pot racks

Elfa Corp. of America, Inc.
601 Ewing Street, B7
Princeton, New Jersey 08540
(609) 683-0660
vinyl-coated wire storage organizers

Gaggenau USA Corp.
5 Commonwealth Avenue
Woburn, Massachusetts 01801
(617) 938-1655
range hoods

Garrett Wade Co.
161 Sixth Avenue
New York, New York 10013
(212) 807-1155
reproduction brass hardware

Gamble Brothers
PO Box 14504
Louisville, Kentucky 40214
(502) 366-0341
cabinet door and drawer replacement system

Grayline Housewares
1616 Berkley Street
Elgin, Illinois 60123
(312) 695-3900
vinyl-coated wire storage organizers

Historic Housefitters
Farm to Market Road
Brewster, New York 10509
(914) 278-2427
traditional wrought-iron and brass hardware

Lyn Hovey Studio, Inc.
266 Concord Avenue
Cambridge, Massachusetts 02138
(617) 492-6566
custom-made stained and leaded glass windows,
walls, doors, lighting fixtures

Hunter Fan Co.
2500 Frisco Avenue
Memphis, Tennessee 38114
(901) 743-1360
ceiling fans

Lightolier/Genlyte
100 Lighting Way
Secaucus, New Jersey 07094-0508
(201) 864-3000
built-in lighting, track lighting, ceiling and wall
fixtures, chandeliers

NuTone, Inc.
Madison & Red Bank Roads
Cincinnati, Ohio 45227
(513) 527-5100
range hoods, exhaust fans, built-in ironing center,
ceiling fans, built-in appliance center

Pittway
780 McClure Road
Aurora, Illinois 60504
(312) 851-7330
First Alert brand kitchen fire extinguishers

Progress Lighting
Erie Avenue & G Street
Philadelphia, Pennsylvania 19134
(215) 289-1200
built-in lighting, track lighting, ceiling and wall
fixtures, chandeliers

Schiller and Asmus, Inc.
Box 575
Yemassee, South Carolina 29945
(803) 589-6211
pot racks

Silverton Victorian Millworks
Box 2987
Durango, Colorado 81302
(303) 259-5915
custom-made and stock Victorian and Colonial
moldings in pine and oak

Stanley Hardware
Division of The Stanley Works
195 Lake Street
New Britain, Connecticut 06050
(203) 225-5111
decorative cabinet hardware, shelf hardware,
sliding drawer hardware

Thomas Industries
Residential Lighting Division
PO Box 7849, Suite 400
7400 LaGrange Road
Louisville, Kentucky 40222
(502) 426-4960
built-in track lighting and fixtures

Tremont Nail Co.
PO Box 111
Wareham, Massachusetts 02571
(617) 295-0038
reproductions of old-fashioned handmade nails

ASSOCIATIONS

Association of Home Appliance Manufacturers
20 N. Wacker Drive
Chicago, Illinois 60606
(312) 984-5800

National Association of the Remodeling Industry
1901 N. Moore Street
Suite 808
Arlington, Virginia 22209
(703) 276-7600

National Kitchen & Bath Association
124 Main Street
Hackettstown, New Jersey 07840
(201) 852-0033

National Kitchen Cabinet Association
PO Box 6830
Falls Church, Virginia 22046
(703) 237-7580

American Gas Association
1515 Wilson Boulevard
Arlington, Virginia 22209
(703) 841-8570

INDEX

Accent lighting, 75
Activity centers, 21-31
    bar/entertaining center, 29, 31
    clean-up center, 21, 27-28
    cooking center, 21, 23-25
    eating center, 21, 29, 31
    food preparation center, 25-26
    menu planning center, 21, 29-30
    refrigerated foods center, 21, 28-29
    serving center, 26-27
    traffic patterns, 23, 24
    work triangle, 22-23
American Institute of Architects, 77
Appliances, 9, 26, 27, 37
    resources for, 83-85
    selection of, 38-56
Architects, 76-77

Barbecues, 47-48
Bar/entertaining center, 29, 31
Base cabinets, 58-61
Bids, 82
Blueprints (working drawings), 16
Bottom-mount refrigerator/freezers, 51
Brick floors, 70
Budget, 80-82
Butcher block, 73
Butcher's racks, 65

Cabinets, 33, 57-65, 77-78
    base, 58-61
    double access, 63
    resources for, 86-87
    specialty, 62-63
    tall, 64
    wall, 61-62
Ceilings, 73-74
Ceramic countertop tile, 72-73
Ceramic floor tile, 69
Ceramic wall tile, 69
Chest freezers, 52, 53
Cleanup center, 21, 27-28
Commercial gas ranges, 41-42
Computers, 30
Convection cooking, 43, 45
Conventional electrical coil cooktops, 45
Convertible cooktops, 47
Cooking center, 21, 23-25
Cooking profile, 12-13
Cooktops, 21, 24, 25
    selection of, 45-47

Cork floors, 70
Cornell University, 22, 23
Corridor (two-wall) kitchens, 32, 33-34
Corridor space, 26, 31
Countertops, 11
    height of, 29, 30, 32
    lighting, 75
    space, 24-27
    types of, 72-73

Dishwashers, 21, 27, 28, 31, 37
    selection of, 54-55
Double-access cabinets, 63

Eating center, 21, 29, 31
Electric cooktops, 45-47
Electric ranges, 40
Electric wall ovens, 42-43
Entertaining profile, 13
Entertainment center, 29, 31
Exhaust hoods, 48-49
Expenses, allocating, 80-82

Faucets, 53-54
Floor plan, 15-20
Floors, 69-72
Fluorescent lighting, 74
Food preparation center, 25-26
Freezers, 21, 28-29
    selection of, 49-52
French-door refrigerator/freezers, 51

Garbage disposals, 27
    selection of, 56
Gas cooktops, 47
Gas-fired barbecues, 47-48
Gas ranges, 39-42
Gas wall ovens, 47
General contractors, 78-79
General lighting, 74-75
Glass-ceramic cooktops, 45, 46
Glazed tile, 70
Greenhouses, 92

Hardwood flooring, 71-72
Hibachi, 48
High-low range, 41
Home Ventilating Institute, 48

Ice makers, 29, 31, 37, 50, 51
Incandescent lighting, 74
Induction cooktops, 45, 46-47

Intercoms, 30
Islands, 32, 35, 37

Kitchen and Bath Show, 38
Kitchen designers, 77-78
Kitchen profiles, 10-13

Layouts, 9, 32-37
    corridor kitchens, 32, 33-34
    islands, 32, 35, 37
    L-shaped kitchens, 32, 34-36
    one-wall kitchens, 32-33
    peninsulas, 32, 34, 35
    U-shaped kitchens, 32, 36-37
Lazy Susan cabinets, 62
Lighting, 9-10, 74-75, 93
    accent, 75
    general, 74-75
    task, 75
Linoleum floors, 70
L-shaped kitchens, 32, 34-36

Marble floors, 70
Meal-time profile, 13
Measuring, 16-20
Menu-planning center, 21, 29-30
Microwave ovens, 21, 23
    selection of, 43-45
Modular refrigerator/freezers, 51-52

National Association of Home Builders
    (NAHB) Show, 38
National Kitchen and Bath Association, 78

One-wall (pullman) kitchens, 32-33
Open storage, 63, 65

Paint, 66-67
Paneling, 68
Pantry, 27
Parquet, 71
Patio doors, 92
Pavers, 70
Peninsulas, 32, 34, 35
Personal profile, 11-12
Plastic laminate, 72
Plumbing fixtures:
    resources for, 87-89
    (See also specific appliances)
Pot racks, 65

Quarry tile, 69-70

Ranges, 21, 23-25
  layouts and, 33-36
  selection of, 39-42
Refrigerated foods center, 21, 28-29
Refrigerators, 23, 28-29, 31
  layouts and, 33, 34
  selection of, 49-52
Resources, 14-15
  directory of, 83-94

Sample expenses, 81
Scrapbooks, 9-10
Serving center, 26-27
Sheet vinyl, 70-71
Side-by-side refrigerator/freezers, 50
Sinks, 21, 23, 27, 28
  layouts and, 32-34, 36
  selection of, 52-54
Slate floors, 70
Solid element (disc) cooktops, 45-46
Solid synthetic countertops, 73
Specialty cabinets, 62-63
Stainless steel countertops, 73
Stone countertops, 73

Storage, 9, 57-65
  base cabinets, 58-61
  calculating needs, 57-58
  choosing cabinets, 58
  open storage, 63, 65
  specialty cabinets, 62-63
  tall cabinets, 64
  wall cabinets, 61-62
Store displays, 14
Structural profile, 10-11
Subcontractors, 78, 79
Surfaces, 10, 66-74
  ceilings, 73-74
  countertops, 72-73
  floors, 69-72
  resources for, 89-91
  walls, 66-69
Sweet's Catalog, 15
Symbols, floor plan, 19

Tall cabinets, 64
Task lighting, 75
Templates, 18-20
Tiles, 69-73
Toaster ovens, 21, 23

Top-mount refrigerator/freezers, 49-50
Traffic patterns, 9, 23, 24
Trash compactors, 27, 28
  selection of, 55-56

U-shaped kitchens, 32, 36-37

Ventilating hoods, 37, 48
Vinyl flooring, 70-71

Wall and rack displays, 12
Wall cabinets, 61-62
Wall coverings, 67
Wall-mounted exhaust hoods, 48-49
Wall ovens, 21, 24
  selection of, 42-43, 47
Wall paneling, 68
Walls, 66-69
Wall tiles, 69
Windows, 92-93
Wood countertops, 73
Work triangle, 22-23, 32, 33

Yellow Pages, 15

METRIC CONVERSION TABLE

Some measurements, particularly on European materials, are given in metric terms. Use this chart to convert metric to U.S. equivalents or U.S. terms to metric equivalents.

To change	To	Multiply by
Inches	Centimeters	2.54
Centimeters	Inches	0.3937
Feet	Meters	0.3048
Meters	Feet	3.2808

CABINETS

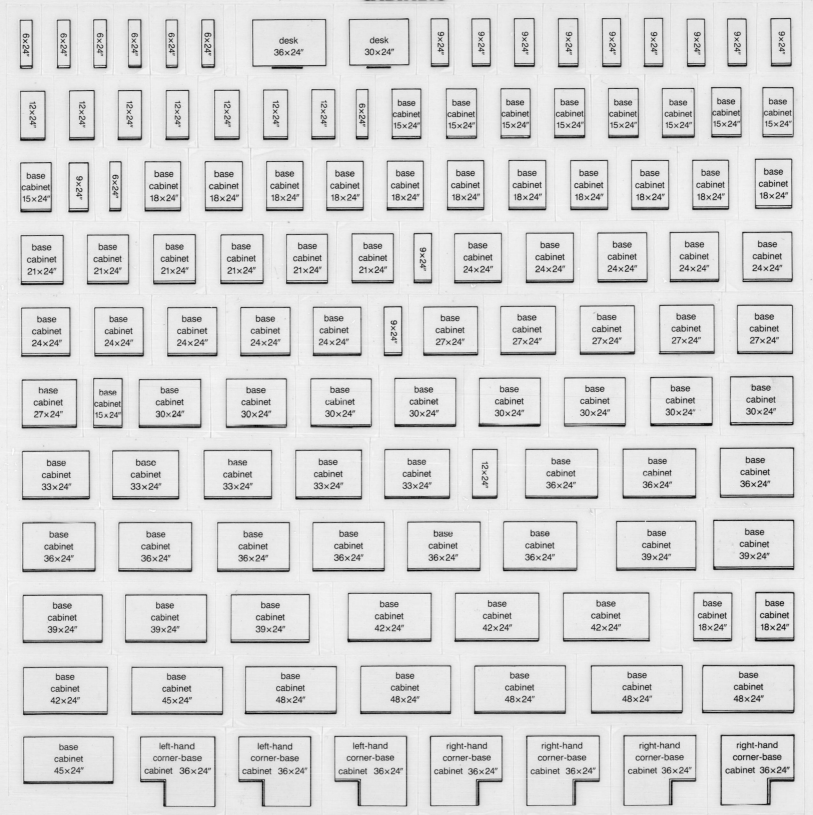

PANTRY CABINETS

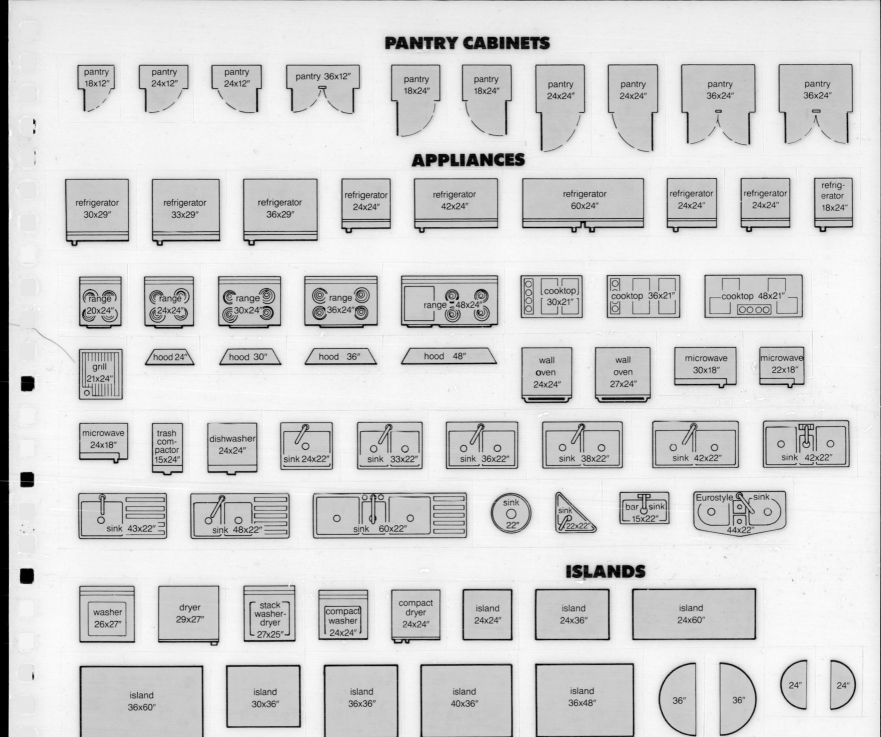

pantry 18x12"
pantry 24x12"
pantry 24x12"
pantry 36x12"
pantry 18x24"
pantry 18x24"
pantry 24x24"
pantry 24x24"
pantry 36x24"
pantry 36x24"

APPLIANCES

refrigerator 30x29"
refrigerator 33x29"
refrigerator 36x29"
refrigerator 24x24"
refrigerator 42x24"
refrigerator 60x24"
refrigerator 24x24"
refrigerator 24x24"
refrigerator 18x24"

range 20x24"
range 24x24"
range 30x24"
range 36x24"
range 48x24"
cooktop 30x21"
cooktop 36x21"
cooktop 48x21"

grill 21x24"
hood 24"
hood 30"
hood 36"
hood 48"
wall oven 24x24"
wall oven 27x24"
microwave 30x18"
microwave 22x18"

microwave 24x18"
trash compactor 15x24"
dishwasher 24x24"
sink 24x22"
sink 33x22"
sink 36x22"
sink 38x22"
sink 42x22"
sink 42x22"

sink 43x22"
sink 48x22"
sink 60x22"
sink 22"
sink 22x22"
bar sink 15x22"
Eurostyle sink 44x22"

ISLANDS

washer 26x27"
dryer 29x27"
stack washer-dryer 27x25"
compact washer 24x24"
compact dryer 24x24"
island 24x24"
island 24x36"
island 24x60"

island 36x60"
island 30x36"
island 36x36"
island 40x36"
island 36x48"
36"
36"
24"
24"

COUNTERTOPS